THE SELF
AND ITS SHEATHS

Owing to the antiquity and rarity of this book, certain pages are regrettably absent, and readability is compromised due to the blurring of the original text. If you possess any insights regarding the availability of these missing sections, kindly inform us. Your assistance is crucial in ensuring the completion of this significant work for the benefit of future generations.

THE SELF AND ITS SHEATHS

ANNIE BESANT

GYAN

Published by

Gyan Publishing House
5, Ansari Road
Daryaganj, New Delhi-110002
Phone: 011-47034999, 9811692060
E-mail: books@gyanbooks.com

Distribution Network
gyanbooks.com
India, USA, Canada, UK, Australia

ISBN: 978-93-6780-945-7 (HB)

First Published, 1895

2nd Impression 2024

Printed at: Gyan Press, Delhi.

THE SELF AND ITS SHEATHS
Author: ANNIE BESANT

THE SELF AND ITS SHEATHS.

FOUR LECTURES

Delivered at the Nineteenth Anniversary

OF THE

THEOSOPHICAL SOCIETY AT ADYAR, MADRAS,

DECEMBER 25TH, 26TH, 27TH, AND 28TH, 1894,

BY

ANNIE BESANT.

BENARES.

THEOSOPHICAL PUBLISHING SOCIETY.

MADRAS: THEOSOPHIST OFFICE, ADYAR.
LONDON: THEOSOPHICAL PUBLISHING SOCIETY, 7, DUKE STREET, ADELPHI, W. C.

1895.

CONTENTS.

PAGE.

The Self and Its Sheaths.

To know man is to know God. To know God is to know man. To study the universe is to learn both God and man; for the universe is the expression of the Divine Thought, and the universe is mirrored in man. Speaking to you last year I spoke of the Kosmos and its building, and speaking to you this year I take the same thought in its essence, but in a new presentment. This time I speak to you of the "SELF and Its Sheaths," of that which understood makes all problems soluble, that which realized clears all difficulties away, that which known brings us to the Supreme Peace, that beyond which there is nothing, and in knowing which we know everything that is or can be.

In these Convention meetings of ours you must remember there is a double purpose; we are here for the work of the Theosophical Society, that presently in our hands must be accomplished; and also we are here for the spiritual side of that mighty movement, for the understanding of ourselves and of the world, in order that by knowledge we may help, by understanding we may guide; and in these mornings, apart from the business portion of our work, we are to consider this mighty problem of the SELF, to try to gain some glimpses as to the SELF in the sheaths in which It is clothed, so that thus studying we may learn the Supreme Secret, and knowing the Supreme Secret may do our duty in the battle of the outer world. For so taught us Shrî Krishna at Kurukshetra; there the Bhagavad Gîtâ was spoken, there the Supreme Secret was unveiled—not to the hermit, not to the recluse, not to the man apart from the haunts of men, but to Arjuna the prince and the warrior, to Arjuna the worker and the struggler; to him for his guidance was the supreme knowledge given; to him, for his helping ere the battle, the truth about the SELF was told.

Last year I pointed out to you three lines of study, three rays of light which, brought together to a single point, illuminated what was obscure, made clear what was difficult. The first of those rays of light came from the Shâstras, came from the spiritual teachings, came from the Supreme Word that is the spiritual source of knowledge; then I pointed out to you that those great Teachers of the past, Who had given the Shâstras for the guiding of the people, had in these latter days sent a Messenger to deal with these same questions in different fashion, and in philosophical and intellectual language to give us the key that had been lost, to give us once more the solutions that had largely disappeared; and then I showed you also that from Western Science, with its observation of the physical universe, with its record of physical phenomena, we might gain another ray of light, and joining this to the other two, taking side by side the spiritual teachings that are the holiest, the intellectual explanations that are necessary for the day, and the science which in scrutinizing the physical universe translates by way of the senses the word of the Supreme Life, that in that way we might gain a knowledge more accurate, an understanding more complete, than if we rejected any one of the three, than if we confined ourselves to the light shed by any one of the rays. I follow the same plan this year. I take as the source of the spiritual teaching those books that are most ancient and most sacred, those books that are the very "Word" given to man; that Science of Brahman which is hidden for us in the Upanishads, and is there, if we can find it, for the guiding of our feet. I take to help us in our study the writings of H. P. Blavatsky, who based herself on those ancient teachings, and cast light upon them from the Secret Knowledge; and I take also to aid us those discoveries of Western Science that give us in concrete form the abstract truth, so that understanding the universe on its physical side we may catch something of the Divine Word, of the truth of ourselves and of the all; and thus I hope to help you, I hope to lead you into some understanding of the SELF, some comprehension of the sheaths in which It is enwrapped. And let me say, that no misunderstanding may arise, why I go back to the ancient writings instead of to the later philosophical schools. There is a mighty name in Indian literature, the name of Shri Shankarâchârya, that no man can name without reverence for the subtlety of his intellect, for the vast range of his intelligence. What was his work? he came in the Kaliyuga, he came when the world was losing or had lost most of its spiritual light, he came to build up round the Science of Brahman the buttress of the intellect, the walls of subtle argumentation, the defences that should be strong and mighty, on which the intellect of the world might break its teeth in vain. And he did it in order that behind that wall of intellectual subtlety, behind that fortress of keen intellectual argument, the Supreme Truth might remain unoutraged by assault, might remain for those who were worthy, might be protected for the spiritual mind. If you take as an example the Brahma Sûtras, with the commentary upon them of Shankarâchârya, you will see exactly what I mean. In his commentary there is the most refined hair-splitting; in his commentary the most subtle distinctions; in his commentary the most careful guarding of language, and the shading of every possible delicacy of thought; and behind all that commentary the Sûtras themselves. If you want to gain their inner essence, if you want them not for intellectual arguments outside, but for the feeding of the Soul within, then take the Sûtras alone in their original tongue, in their own unadorned form, and in silent meditation, when the senses are quiet and when the mind is tranquil, when the light of the SELF is shining—then take a Sûtra and listen to it in its own words alone, and you will learn a spiritual truth that no argument may avail to reach.

And now let us try and look backward into what to us is the past; let us go to the beginning of a universe, and try to realise what is meant by the SELF; for the SELF of the universe and the SELF of man are one, and in knowing the SELF we know That which is at the root of the universe and of man alike. Thus travelling backward to the beginning, we come to an infinite Darkness where there is no thought, no language, where nothing human nor limited may be. It has no name, no words may describe It; nothing that can be said of THAT but is utterly mistaken; and when the writers of old had gone backwards and backwards, when they had reached Brahman Who is without origin, Who is the One and the All, then in face of the silence beyond and the darkness, they used one epithet only to describe It: It is beyond Brahman, It is Supreme Brahman, Parabrahman! and there all voice is silent, all thought falls dead.

But as we try in thought to watch the Darkness before the universe is born, by an effort of the imagination placing ourselves where there is nothing, where everything is as it were emptiness and space, then as standing in the darkness of the night and looking skyward into the darkness, there might glimmer through the darkness a light which is formless, we know not whence it comes nor how, save that where there was blackness of darkness there now is a glimmering that foretells the coming of the sun—so in that emptiness which is all-fullness, in that darkness indescribable by us, there is a glimmer, there is light without form, says the Scripture, luminousness that has no shape, light that is only light without limitation, and on that glimmering light for a moment our thought may rest, for *there* is the first point where thought is possible at all ; and then we hear sounding forth those sublime words of the *Mundakopanishad :*

> Luminous without form......without origin, without life, without mind.*

Without life ? without mind ? what mean these strange words of the Origin of all life and mind ? He *has* nothing ; nay, He *is* nothing ; He, out of Whom springs the root of all that shall be, out of THAT which has and is nothing—no special thing just because it is the source of all the not yet unfolded possibilities of everything that shall be—out of THAT a universe is to be builded, out of THAT all that shall be is to come. But there is no mind—why not ? Because mind implies more than the One, and THAT is one ; because mind implies separation, and here there is no separateness ; because mind implies some one that is thinking, and something that is thought of, and there is as yet but the One in Whom is enfolded all that may be thought but has not yet come into manifestation. Therefore rightly and wisely in dealing with this subject, and in throwing it into the intellectual form which is necessary if our thought is to be in any sense understood on earth, therefore rightly and wisely, Madame Blavatsky—in dealing with this which is beyond all consciousness, with this which is beyond mind, with this which is beyond thought, not because it is less but because it is so much more, because it is deeper, wider, all-embracing—says :

> Being Absolute Consciousness and Absolute Motion—to the limited

* ii, 2.

senses of those who describe this indescribable—it is unconsciousness and immovableness. Concrete consciousness cannot be predicated of abstract consciousness, any more than the quality wet can be predicated of water—wetness being its own attribute, and the cause of the wet quality in other things. Consciousness implies limitations and qualifications ; something to be conscious of and some one to be conscious of it. . . We call Absolute Consciousness "unconsciousness," because it seems to us that it must necessarily be so, just as we call the Absolute "Darkness," because to our finite understanding it appears quite impenetrable ; yet we recognise fully that our perception of such things does not do them justice. We involuntarily distinguish in our minds, for instance, between unconscious Absolute Consciousness and unconsciousness, by secretly endowing the former with some indefinite quality that corresponds, on a higher plane than our thoughts can reach, with what we know as consciousness in ourselves. But this is not any kind of consciousness that we can manage to distinguish from what appears to us as unconsciousness. *

So again she quotes from the Divine Pymander :

God is not a mind, but the cause that the Mind is ; not a spirit, but the cause that the Spirit is ; not light, but the cause that the Light is. †

Let us try to realize what this means. The mind of man thinks, but in order to think it must remember the Past, it must realize the Present, it must look forward to the Future. But in Brahman there is no Past, nor Present, nor Future ; there is one eternal Now, and no distinguishment of time, of place, of succession of states. Therefore a great Teacher is quoted in this connexion, as baffled by the limitations of human thought and language :

---

* *Secret Doctrine,* vol. i., pp. 86, 87.
† *Ibid,* p. 305.

As said in the Scriptures : "The Past Time is the Present Time, as also the Future, which though it has not come into existence still is" ... Our ideas, in short, on duration and time are all derived from our sensations according to the laws of association. Inextricably bound up with the relativity of human knowledge, they nevertheless can have no existence except in the experience of the individual Ego, and perish when its evolutionary march dispels the Mâyâ of phenomenal existence. What is time, for instance, but the panoramic succession of our states of consciousness ? In the words of a Master : "I feel irritated at having to use these three clumsy words—Past, Present and Future ; miserable concepts of the objective phases of the subjective whole, they are about as ill-adapted for the purpose as an axe for fine carving."*

In that eternal Now, no thought, as we know thought, is possible ; in that eternal Present, no distinctions as we make them can exist ; and therefore Brahman is "without mind," because He is above it. And then the Scripture goes on to say that out of Him come life and mind and all ; so that that First and Supreme, the One out of Which everything is to be builded, that is Brahman, the SELF of the Universe, it is Ishvara, the Lord.

And now what is the next step? Again from the Sacred Writings, I take the words that are to guide us :

It willed : I will multiply. †

There is the beginning of the universe ; there the commencement of differentiation ; and it is an internal differentiation and not an external expansion ; it is not a change of nature, but a change of condition ; it is not an alteration of substance, but of variety within the One, due to the word, "I will multiply ;" and the very first

---

* *Ibid*, p. 75.

† *Chhândogyopanishad*, vi, II, 3.

stage of this internal differentiation is that which shows itself as Life, said by the Scripture to be "concealed in Name and Form," and then from the Life concealed in Name and Form the Mind comes forth ; so speaks the Scripture. Now let us take it for a moment in the explanation that is given us in the *Secret Doctrine*, and then in Science, which will throw so startling a light on this marvellous far-off stage that you will realise how true it is that the universe is the expression of the Divine Thought. Intellectually put, this differentiation is within the One ; this internal preparation for a universe is put in the form of the three Logoi. I have no time to dilate upon Them, I can only mention Them : The First is the essence of life and the cause of all. The Second is double, spirit-matter, positive-negative, or call it what you like. The Third is Divine Ideation, or power of thought. If you want the details you must go back to the last year's lectures. I have not the time to repeat them.

Now come to Science. Suppose you took a microscope in hand, and suppose that looking through the microscope you took the first germ of living matter out of which a plant or an animal was to grow, you would see beneath your eyes under the microscope a tiny speck of matter, and in that speck of matter a single spot ; as you watched the speck of matter and the central spot within it, you would slowly become conscious—you could not say when it began, you would be unable to say exactly when first you were able to see it—but by slow change imperceptible in the beginning and only becoming perceptible gradually, as you watch through the great magnifying power of the glass, you would see in the central spot a separation, and you would see towards each end of the speck of matter two spots appearing ; you would see within this one speck of matter and the central spot a slow strange gathering together of the material substance, until this change would appear when complete : that instead of one you had two, and these two apart at the two poles, as they are called, of this little mass of matter. So that you would have two separate distinct spots, duality where there had been unity, separation internally where there had been none. You would see the two poles within one mass. Those poles are different though they look the same. Out of the same substance —for there was only one—by internal differentiation two separate and yet not separated bodies have formed. How do I know they are different, you may ask. Because action takes place between them ; because between those two poles lines are set up, shapes appear ; because between the two poles of the speck of matter there is alteration, there is variety, there is differentiation, there are more and more distinct marks of interchanging action ; thus it comes to pass that the one is recognized as positive, the other is recognised as negative ; and between the two everything formative occurs, and there is built up the germ of the coming plant ; then the plant grows and differentiates further, and develops into three, and you have your root, your stock and your leaves ; but all these formed in germ between the two poles that were one and then two. Most marvellous picture in the concrete of the differentiation in the Supreme. Between the two poles a universe is builded, and out of duality the whole variety comes forth; therefore it is that we read that after the One has given birth to the Two, after the Life has become Name and Form, then comes the Mind, then comes Ideation, then comes the Divine Thought, the picture of all that shall be, and the image of the universe that not yet has come to the birth. For this is the womb of Brahman of which Shrî Krishna spake. This is the eternal womb from which the universe shall proceed and the Third—Mahat, if you call it so, the Third Logos if you call it so, Shrî Krishna if you call it so—is the eternal Father, that puts the seed within the womb out of which all else shall come. This is the manifestation of the universe within the Divine Form, and therefore you read in the 11th portion of *Bhagavad Gîtâ* of the time when the four-armed Krishna appeared in His Divine Form stretching from earth to sky, blazing as a thousand suns, before the dazzled eyes of Arjuna, and when Arjuna—gifted with the divine eye that alone might gaze into that splendour that no mortal eye could face, no mortal mind might grasp—cried out in his ecstasy: "In Thy body I see all the Gods, and all the gradations of living things." For all is within the Divine Thought as Idea, before it is born as Form, and before it comes into manifestation it is stored in the treasure-house of the Universal Mind.

Therefore is it written that for the sake of the SELF everything is dear: not for the outer shape but for the inner SELF—the lowest as well as the highest, the speck of dirt as well as the loftiest Deva. Brahman is in all, pervades all ; everything is there. Face the imperfection of the universe, and there you will find the supreme consolation. If there is to be a universe, there must be limitation ; if there is limitation, there must be less than perfection, *i.e.*, imperfection ; if there is imperfection, then only you can have variety ; but the separated things cannot be perfect, since perfection belongs to the unlimited and the all. Then if a universe is to be built at all, imperfection must appear. The limits of the imperfection are the limits of the variety. That means, in our mortal words, that there must be evil as well as good. Evil is only imperfection, and where limitation is, evil, as we call it, must needs exist. Give the separated things self-moving power and there will be the striking of one against another, till each obeys the law of the whole ; and because in a universe there must be variety, therefore Shrî Krishna said : " I am the dice of the gambler" as much as He is the purity of the righteous. You cannot separate one single thing from the Supreme ; It is the SELF of all, and exists in all, and is all. Then, indeed, further differentiation ; then, indeed, though all be Itself, all becomes apparently separate and even in conflict. Strange paradox ! Let me see if again from Science I can gain an analogy which may help you. When the solar system is going to be built a great nebula appears—a mist of fire. That fire-mist has in it everything that in the solar system is going to be gradually evolved; within that fire-mist is everything in essence that the system can show. Presently a mass of fiery vapour is hurled from the central mass. It is a planet, it is a future world, and as this process goes on, planet after planet is hurled from the central mass yet continues to revolve around it, until at last you have a sun in the centre and planets circling all round. They are the same as the sun in their essence; all are of the whirling fire-mist that was unseparated in the beginning; but now it has become a sun that gives light to separated planets; although they are all the same in essence, there is a difference in condition. The analogy is not perfect, but it may help us, and so it is written that as one sun illuminates the whole world, so one Self is in every separated body.* But all is Itself.

You remember the story of Uddâlaka, who taught his son by salt dissolved in water. You remember how he made the boy take the salt and put it into the water, and how the next day he asked for it back again, and the boy said he could not find it. Then the father said: "Taste from the top of the water;" and the son said: "it is saltish;" and the father said: "taste from the middle of the water," and the son said: "it is saltish;" and the father said: "Taste from the bottom of the water," and the son said: "it is saltish." Then the father told his son that as the salt which could not be seen yet pervaded all, so it was with Brahman, the Universal Soul. All-pervading, omnipresent, eternal, the root, the life, the

* *Bhag. Gîtâ,* xiii, 33.

essence, the substance of all, one and indivisible in substance, separate in the manifested sheaths that It is going of Its own substance to evolve ; whatever is exists and lives by It, the SELF of the universe, THAT from which everything proceeds. And then Uddâlaka gave a bridge from the One to the many. He had taught his son that the salt was everywhere in the water though it had disappeared from sight ; he had taught him that the universe was pervaded by the One. And then he spake the words : "It is the Universal SELF. O Svetaketu ! thou art THAT." There is our bridge : thou art Atmâ, and Atmâ and Brahman are one. In the heart of men there is a cavity, and there is Brahman to be found hidden, the SELF of man, the SELF of the universe. If we speak of the SELF of man, we sometimes say Atmâ ; then we say Paramâtmâ of the SELF of all ; if we say of man Purusha, then we say Purushottama of the SELF of all. But It is one and the same everywhere, in the great and in the small ; there is no difference, there is no separation, there is one eternal undying and ancient SELF, and that SELF is the SELF in you and in me. There may be difference in condition in manifestation, but the essence and the nature is one and the same ; and therefore is it written in that most marvellous of all Upanishads, the *Chhândogya*, the mightiest and most mystical of all, the hardest to unravel and to understand ; therefore is it written in the *Chhândogyopanishad* that Atmâ is the bridge.

Crossing that bridge the blind no longer are blind, the wounded no longer are wounded, the sorrowful no longer sorrow. Therefore crossing that bridge, nights verily become as days. Eternally radiant is that place of Brahman.*

And so again is it written in the *Mundakopanishad* :

Cease from words ; He is the bridge to immortality. †

Now "He" is Brahman, dwelling in the secret place, in the cavity of the heart, for Atmâ and Brahman are one, and in finding the SELF we find Brahman.

Let us take our next stage. I turn to the same great Scripture. I take from it further words, for our next step is so difficult, so little understood, that out of the want of understanding grow the many controversies of the schools, and the continual arguments which divide intellect from intellect. Let us then take the simple words first, and then let us work them out. It is written in the same *Chhândogyopanishad :*

He who willeth; "I shall smell," He is Atmâ, desiring to smell odours ; He who willeth, "I shall speak," He is Atmâ, desiring to utter words ; He who willeth, "I shall hear," He is Atmâ, desiring to hear sounds ; He who willeth, "I shall think," He is Atmâ ; Manas is the divine eye. ‡

Yet again we remember how we have read that desire awaked in the bosom of the Eternal and gave birth to manifestation, § and again that the "nature of Purusha is desire."‖ How shall we reconcile the paradox ? How shall we understand the seeming contradiction that Atmâ is at once the witness and the agent—is at once quiescent and active—is at once not doing and doing—

---

* viii, IV., 1, 2.

† ii, 5.

‡ viii, XII, 4, 5.

§ *Secret Doctrine,* vol. ii., p. 185.

‖ Brihadâranyopanishad (Bombay Edition) iv, IV, 5. Purusha is here *embodied* soul.

is at once the changeless, immutable, and yet the only agent in the universe of manifested things? If we can understand this, ah! then our road opens before us. Here the crux of our difficulty—here the great problem that we must now endeavour to solve. As Atmâ, Atmâ is quiescent; as Atmâ, Atmâ is immovable; as Atmâ, Atmâ is the witness; as Atmâ, Atmâ does nothing, and acts not. What then means the Scripture when it says that Atmâ doeth all these things? As Atmâ—other than Which there is nothing—wills within Itself, so does It make out of Its own substance that which we call the sheaths. Those sheaths are Itself, for there is naught else, but they are differentiations within Itself, changed conditions due to Its own will: "I will multiply", in which It is active and in which It does the many things of which the Scripture speaks. In Its own nature, changeless, unacting, in the sheaths It is the actor; not out of the sheath, but in the sheath; not separated from the sheath, but working in the sheath; so that while in Itself it moveth not, in the sheaths It moveth everything that is—in the sheath, that for the purpose It hath brought out of Itself into manifestation. Therefore do we speak of all as Mâyâ, because there is but the One Reality, out of Which by thought everything proceeds, because out of Itself by will all goes forth. But to you and to me who look from the outside, that is from the sheath, there is difference, because we see the sheath and see not the Atmâ, that is concealed by Name and Form; for in one sheath It is will, in another sheath It is desire, in another sheath It is living activity, in another sheath It is chemical attraction and repulsion, and It is all the wondrous forces in the Universe; but the difference is in the sheath and not in the One that is; in the changed conditions of manifestation, and not in the manifesting Life. If I take a current of electricity and if I send it through water charged with a solution of silver, down will fall the silver, and that falling will be the result of the invisible current; and if I carry the current onward into a narrow wire—a thin wire—out of the wire will shine the light, and that will be the effect of the same current; in the one case the difference of condition throws down a solid; in another case the difference of condition gives forth a light. It is one electric force in both the cases, and the difference of manifestation lies in that in which it is working and not in itself. The analogy is imperfect, as it must be; it may yet help us to understand how one may be manifested in many ways, how there is one Atmâ in substance, but multiplicity by changed conditions that we call sheaths.

It is again written * that though the body be mortal, it is the dwelling place of Atmâ, and that in the sheaths Atmâ comes into contact with desirable and repulsive objects, while out of the sheaths It comes not into touch with aught; and because while in the sheaths It comes into contact with all that is around, It becomes subject to these contacts. The outgoing energy is Atmâ; the sheath makes the difference in manifestation. Thus we shall begin to understand.

* Chhândogya, viii, xii, 1.

This is the point at which I shall have to leave my subject this morning to take it up to-morrow; this is the point I want you now to realise and carry away, because on this depends the understanding of everything that follows: Atmâ, giving out of Itself everything that is to be, works in these differentiated selves in different ways. It works to make the material of a material universe; in the atom It works to build up the physical substratum (which is Itself), works to bring about a particular result; so that one line of this manifesting energy is going to be the building up of physical atoms which are to be used for the physical universe, for the physical body of man, for the whole line of Prâkritic evolution, in this and every region of the universe. That is the evolution of form, of everything that has extension; it may be physical, it may be astral, it may belong to the world of Kâma, desire, it may belong to the world of Manas, thought. Nay, it may belong to the very region of Buddhi, and yet it will be a sheath—that is it will have form, it will have as it were extension; that is, it will serve for the purpose of manifestation, which necessitates the existence of form. And you will remember that five sheaths are given: the highest is Anandamayakosha, bliss sheath, Buddhi; then coming downwards there is the sheath for higher Manas, the Vignânamayakosha; then for lower Manas and Kâma, the Manomayakosha, for all manifestations of working intellect and desire; and yet another for Prâna; and another the food sheath, the Annamayakosha, which is made of the physical material of the universe. These are the sheaths and all have to be builded by the One. In the building of the sheaths lies difference of manifestation. In that the change of forms, in that the activity which is going to make the whole sheath-side of the universe and of man. But that is not all ; there is another side of the activity which goes to the building up, by means of the sheath, of the individual man ; no longer now only the Atmâ in essence, that is the One ; no longer now only the sheath in its separable materials of the Form side ; there is the Name, the inner man, the individual, that which is going to pass from birth to birth, that which is going to gather experience, that which is going to learn, and by learning know ; that which is going to become the individual mind of man, which is going to be built up by life and death, by birth and decay, by passing into Svarga and by coming back from Svarga into new birth ; by these births and deaths is going to be built up into a mirror of the All ; it is going to become the individual Self which is and shall be, which has its own knowledge and has its own distinguishment ; it is that of which Shrî Krishna said : " It is unborn and constant and eternal", because in its essence it is Atmâ Itself, and yet it is also that which experienced births and deaths, though itself neither born nor dying. Shrî Krishna looking back knew all His former births and remembered the events of each ; Arjuna had been born many times although he knew it not. And you and I have been born many times before, and before us also births and deaths may spread. That is the building up of the individual. That is the building up by the sheaths, which is slowly accomplished. So that we leave it at this point: One SELF, Atmâ, in Itself inactive; sheaths of Its substance in which It is going to act, sheaths builded by It along one line of evolution; and then Atmâ working within the sheaths to build up the individual, the Ego, the self-conscious I—which shall know itself separate in manifestation, although rooted by its origin in the One and the All. Carried on into further detail, this thought will lead us through this tangle, a clue to guide our puzzled steps out of the apparent contradictions of the One and the many, the All which is at once one and manifold; keep that thought for this morning and we will follow it whither it leads us in the mornings that lie in front. But grasp that clearly and everything else will become simple and definite, and we shall learn how our bodies to-day are built of atoms, how these atoms by change shall be built into the living man, how the man of this Manvantara shall become the Deva of another, how step by step this growth is ever proceeding, how in every universe there is Ishvara, how in every one He weaves out of Himself the material basis, how out of the elaborated material basis of past universes He builds the living Egos of men, how out of these He builds the Devas of another universe, and ultimately unites them in Himself, that is the All. Such is the mighty subject on which we are to think for these four mornings of our meeting, the Supreme Secret of the Master, by knowing which all things are known.

The Body of Action.

My brothers: Let me remind you at the outset of the three rays of light which we are going to use in order to illuminate the very difficult subject which lies before us. First, we take the ray of spiritual light which comes to us from the ancient Scriptures, from the Shrutis, and, with limitations, from the Smritis. Then we take the ray of intellectual light which comes to us through H. P. B., giving us the intellectual ladder by which we may rise to the higher region. And then we take the ray that comes from Western Science, examining the physical Universe, and bearing record to the facts that it observes. These are the three, you will remember, that I said yesterday were to be the rays of light converging to a single focus, to illuminate the obscurity that we are trying to pierce. And let me say on Science this; that the thing that we find to-day of opposition between Science and Spiritual Knowledge is a plant of modern growth and does not come from the ancient world. Science in the old days was the hand-maiden of Religion and was not its opponent, and I hope it will be one of the glories of Theosophy to bring back Science to its real duty, as showing on the sensuous plane what Religion shows on the spiritual; once more the child and the servant, once more the helper and the buttress of the Wisdom-Religion of old.

Now the section of the subject that to-day we have to deal with is, first of all, the object of the sheaths—not worked out; that will be done in my last lecture; but a word or two on the object—in order to show to you how and why there should be sheaths at all. Then something on the becoming of a Universe, for by studying the becoming of the Universe that now is, we shall understand both what the present inherits from the past, and also what it is preparing to bequeath to the future. For in every universe there is a preparation of that which in the next universe shall serve as material. In each universe there is an inheritance from the past of what in the previous universes was prepared for the present. You cannot separate one universe from another, nor deal with a single manifestation as though it were isolated from the rest. There is ever an out-breathing from the One, in-breathing again into the One when a Manvantara is over; out-breathing for a fresh Manvantara, in-breathing again when that also is concluded; but all the out-breathings and the in-breathings are connected. And the out-breathing of to-day has in it results of the in-breathings that have preceded it in time, and therefore to understand we must remember that in every Universe we look backwards for its inheritance, and we look forwards to see what it will lead to; we study the present universe because it is the nearest, and here we can best learn to understand the process of becoming. Then—finishing this brief description of the outline of what I have to say—I shall deal in detail with two of the sheaths, the two lower sheaths, that of Annam or food, and that of Prâna or life. To-morrow morning I shall deal with the two sheaths that belong to the Mental and Emotional activities, with the Manomayakosha and Gnânamayakosha, leaving myself for the last discourse to say the little that can be said on the highest sheath—the Anandamayakosha, and then dealing in detail with the object of the sheaths and the final result which comes out of the whole.

In taking now at once the first division that I have thus sketched of to-day's work—the object of the sheaths—let me remind you, taking up what is written in the *Mundakopanishad* which I quoted yesterday, as to Brahman being "without life, without mind," that then in the very next shloka it is written:

> From Him are produced Life, Mind, and all the organs, ether, air, light, water, earth.*

Purposely—let me say, in parenthesis, I am translating. I am not using here a distinct quotation in Sanskrit from the Sacred Books, and I will tell you frankly my reason. Shlokas which come from the Vedas have in them a Mântric force which may not be used in a mixed assemblage, and may not be raised among the conflicting magnetisms which are gathered together without distinction and without separation. I am using the teaching; I am not using the Sanskrit

* ii, I, 3.

tongue in the definite order of its syllables, which gives them the force of Mantrams. Every quotation that I intend to give to you this morning, I have taken myself in the Sanskrit, so that I may be sure that I am giving the meaning accurately. I am not in any one case going to quote the original, because I will not take on myself the responsibility of repeating the Mantram-form in the mixed audience that I address now.

It is written in the *Mundakopanishad* that from Brahman the One—I need not repeat to you to-day that which I addressed to you yesterday—comes Life—Prâna is the word used. I shall show you presently that Prâna is Atmâ in its outgoing activity; then Mind, Manas, that is the second; then the five elements as we know them—ether, air, fire, water and earth; seven in all. These are the seven regions of the universe; the seven sheaths of Brahman, as the SELF of the All; corresponding to those in Man are the sheaths with which we have now to deal; and the object of the Sheaths in man is to come into contact with each corresponding region in the Universe. So that Atmâ, which in itself is pure Sat and therefore quiescent, so that Atmâ which cannot as Atmâ deal with these different regions by way of contact, may through the sheaths come into contact with everything, and so gradually build up an individual self-consciousness, many individual self-consciousnesses; the building of these individuals is the object of the Universe, and at the end of the Manvantara, of the Universe, there is the existence of these separated self-consciousnesses which were not existent as self-consciousnesses at the beginning, but only existent potentially in the Atmâ, Which is the root of the possibility of all.

Then we come first to our material Universe, as we call it. Let us realize that in this material Universe, in the widest sense of the term, Prakriti, that we have the seven-fold division to which I have just alluded, and that the essence of Matter, not Matter as we have it down here, but the essence of Matter is eternal. Prakriti, says Shrî Krishna, is eternal; not in its manifestation but in its essence; not in its manifestation but in its root; the root of Matter not yet in manifestation, that is eternal in Brahman, or otherwise never could it be. For once again says the Divine Teacher:

> The non-existent cannot become, neither can the existent cease to be.

You must hold firm to the principle that if a thing be true, the outer and superficial difficulties are things to be conquered, without letting go the fundamental truth that you have. Have faith enough in Truth to hold to fact when you have it, and believe that if a thing be a fact it must come into co-ordination with all other truths, and as knowledge increases all superficial difficulties will gradually vanish away. Now this Matter, or Prakriti, which is without beginning in its essence, never can be separated from that which is co-eternal with it, that which comes with it into manifestation, and abides with it for evermore. For you cannot talk of Matter alone. If you say Matter, you must say Spirit. If you say Prakriti, you must say Purusha. They are the two sides of the one existence, and are never to be separated from each other in fact, although in thought we distinguish them by quality, in order that we may be able to think at all. But in manifestation they are never apart. There is no such thing as dead Matter. There is no such thing as Spirit, or force, or life, without Matter by which it takes its form, by which it shows its energy. Wherever there is Name there is Form, wherever there is Form there is Name. Life is hedged round by the two, and they are never separated in manifestation.

Now H. P. Blavatsky in dealing with this points out that Matter *becomes*, and she quotes the teachings of a mighty Egyptian who drew his knowledge from the Rishis of old, and gave out through Egypt to Greece, and so onwards to the Western world, the Eastern teaching, which is the source of all our knowledge on these subjects. And this great Egyptian, Hermes, saying exactly as he had been taught, declared :

"Oh, my son, Matter *becomes*; formerly it *was*; for Matter is the vehicle of becoming.

Realize that idea ; Matter is a "vehicle of becoming ;" and no Universe may be without this vehicle of becoming, as well as the force that informs. And then taking it still more clearly—and here doing us one of those great services that should make her name to be held ever in honor and in respect amongst us—she explains to us what this means. Everything that is, that was, that will be, eternally IS. Even the countless forms in the Universe are finite and perishable only in their objective, and never in their ideal form; they exist as Ideas in the eternity; when they vanish as forms they still exist as reflections. If you realize that, you will understand the links that unite the Universes together. Nothing that ever has been can perish. It exists for ever in the Eternal Thought. Objective existence perishes, the ideal form remains for ever, and is handed on from Manvantara to Manvantara. The objective forms of to-day will be handed on to the next Universe as ideal forms; they are to govern the line of evolution, so that each successive Universe inherits the Karma of the past, as it modifies and builds the Karma of all the Universes yet to be.

Now an atom is at once the form and the force of life. In every Universe the atom is the basis which in that Universe is built for the lowest types of manifestation on every plane; that is, it is the form of every plane. In those seven that I spoke of—the five great Elements, Prâna and Manas—you have in each of these planes this basis of the atom, modified as we come down lower and lower into more and more objective forms, but ever present as the form-side of the region. And this building up of the form-side in the atom is repeated in every Universe, and the atom of one Universe passes on as ideal form to take its place as the life of the line of Evolution of the next. Try to realize that, for it is the key to the puzzle in every Universe of forms involving, and instinct with, life; through the Universe the process of becoming, then passing into the ideal and remaining as reflection in the Eternal One that IS, and coming forth in the next Universe to be the informing life of the atoms of the next. So that in each case that which in one Universe is, to use a clumsy phrase, an outer form becomes in the next an informing life; and the atom of the one is the mind and the energy of the next; and so each Universe is builded and linked to those that in time lie behind.

Now let us see the atom as a form and a force; the Atmâ and in addition the sheath which Atmâ differentiates within Itself for the manifestation of Its own energy; and so it is written in an Esoteric Scripture that

> The Jîvas are the Souls of the atoms.*

Again, I say, try to realize that thought: Jîva is another name for Atmâ in manifestation; Jîva is the Soul of the atom—that is, that in every atom you have this duality; the Atmâ that informs and the differentiated Atmâ which makes Itself the sheath. This is the work of building the Prâkritic side, as it were, of Atmâ.

Again turning to H. P. Blavatsky, we learn that these atoms are "visible complex units" and act *from within*—a point of enormous importance, as you will see when in a moment I pass to what Science tells us about them. For H. P. B. writing on these atoms said, as we have seen, that there are Souls to these atoms, that they are informed with Jîva. And then she goes on to say that these atoms fill the immensity of space, that within the atoms is all the activity, and that the atoms become complex units—note the phrase "every atom

* *Secret Doctrine*, vol. i, p. 679.

becomes a complex unit"—that they propel the molecules into activity from within.*

Now turn to Science. Science deals with atoms in chemical form and also of course in the physical. The chemical form is the one that throws most light on the Occult side of Nature. The physical deals more with the outer manifestation; the chemical deals more with the forces that mould the outer manifestation. Now Western Science dealing chemically with the atom gives us certain facts, and they are very strange. I will take one form of atom in order that what I may say may be distinct, and let me say that if this is difficult to follow, as I know it is, you will have it presently in print, and you can study the technicalities that I cannot avoid when I am dealing with a highly instructed audience, as I have the right to expect this audience to be. I have not the time to explain as I should do to a popular audience. I will take Carbon, an atom of Carbon, in the mineral kingdom. It is a simple thing. It joins other elements and enters into combinations, and it has the power of joining by a four-fold link. If I may appeal for the moment to your imagination, think that you see a Carbon atom ; think of a ball and into that ball four hooked sticks are stuck, so that they leave outside their four hooks. Thus you will have a ball with four hooks sticking out. That is the chemical atom of Carbon in the mineral kingdom. By each of these hooks it can join on to a hook of another chemical atom, so that it can join with four other atoms provided that

* *Ibid*, pp. 679 and 694.

each of these four atoms has only one hook of its own. In the mineral kingdom you may follow that right through, and you may get a number of compounds of different chemical elements in which Carbon plays its part, in which it joins itself with one or the other, in which it unites itself by these hooks—stretching out its hooks as it were, and grasping other elements—but always simple in its combinations, hooking on to two atoms of an element that has two hooks, to four of an element that has one hook, and so on. For when an atom is working in the building of this most material part of the Universe, it is beginning in the simplest way; by a changing of the inner constitution of the atom, it gradually becomes able to enter into more and more complex combinations. Follow on our Carbon atom—remembering it is Atmâ *plus* form—and follow it out from the mineral into the vegetable and animal kingdoms. What is the difference? The difference is that in this Carbon atom there is developed a power of combination in more and more complex ways, so that at last, in what is called Organic Chemistry technically, you get numbers of compounds in which the Carbon atoms unite in what are called technically "closed rings," instead of in lines as in the mineral kingdom. These closed rings of Carbon atoms make up the most complicated combinations of every character, and these are never found in the mineral kingdom, but only when that has been accomplished, and the further evolution has been followed. So that in this working we can see that in the atom there is evolution, in the atom there is change, in the atom there is the differentiating life ; the working of Atmâ in this lower kingdom is to inform this atom, to differentiate it within, to make it more and more complex in its inner powers, so that it may manifest more and more of life, until at last, built through mineral, vegetable and animal kingdoms, it shall be ready to be built into the sheaths of the Man, and there in combination with other similar atoms make the sheath which Atmâ can use gradually for the building of an individual self-consciousness. Thus the atomic building, and the combination of atoms into molecules, and of the molecules then again into cells, and of cells into the sheath, give us the food-sheath hat is necessary for contact with the lowest region of the Universe ; and by this process brings Atmâ into contact, as we shall see later, with the subtle sheaths of the mind, into physical contact with the material universe for the gathering of experience, by contact, by attraction, by repulsion, by pleasure and by pain.

Now supposing that you have been able to follow that, we can come to our first sheath, that of Food—the Annamayakosha, the body that we use, the body that we wear. I am not my body. I need not tell you that this body is not me ; this is a thing that I use for certain purposes ; but it is I who use it.

There is a double activity in this sheath of ours that we call our body. First there is the activity of the atoms and the molecules and the cells of the body. This is not your activity but theirs. Not your activity, but the activity of the Atmâ in the atoms and the molecules and the cells of the body. It is not Atmâ's activity in the sheaths as the Self of the sheath, but Atmâ's activity in the constituent particles as the Self of the particles which is necessary for their existence. How can I prove that to you? By Science once more. See how I can use this Western Science for purposes they dream not of who observe for us the facts. But see how useful is their work! They observe the facts and give them to the world; granted they do not know what the facts imply; granted they do not see the underlying verities. But they see the physical truths and speak the physical truths; and we who are taught by the ancient Teachers can take the physical fact and illuminate it by the Divine Light, and understand the "why" as well as the "how," the cause as well as the effect. So I turn to my Science. The cells in the body, says the great German Materialist, Haeckel, the cells have Souls. Our great Materialist Haeckel has struck on a strange and occult truth. There is, he says, a Soul of the cell. Why does he say this? because he finds in the separate cells of the body here is a cell-activity, that is not the activity of the body as a whole. He finds that the separate cells of the body exercise particular functions of their own, without regard to the general actions of the body. They select, they choose, they accept, they reject, each cell according to its own impulse, each cell according to its own work. But there is this strange peculiarity: that the so to speak independent action of the cell is limited to its own narrow interest, and while it is subordinated in its normal activity to the general welfare of the body of which it forms a part—as you will see when we come to Prâna—none the less is it true that it will sometimes act against the general welfare, following out the law of its own activity and unconscious of the greater use which it serves in the little universe of the body. Take a cut ; you may get a wound in the body. What will the cells do ? They will set to work at once ; without any thought of your brain, without any consciousness of yours, without any directing force of your intelligence, they will bring to that place where matter has been cut away the new supplies that are wanted for the filling up of the hole in the body that has been left. They will build and build and build ; and they will build without the intelligence which should subordinate their building to the whole ; for they will make a scar, they will build more than is wanted. For what the physiologists call the "unconscious memory of the cell" makes the building go on, building and building and building beyond the point that is necessary, following out their individual activity by the law of their own nature, and not conscious of the needs of the greater one that they are clothing. So that you get your scar which you cannot get rid of. So also you get continually built matter which then is flung away, and the whole activity of the outer cells of your body is continually building matter that then is thrown off again. For they build and build and build according to the law of their own activity, by the Atmâ in the cell building the cell, and not considering the need of the sheath as a complicated whole.

But here is an important thing to learn. There is an "I" as well as a sheath, and the "I" uses this sheath for its own purpose. The "I" in me wants to write. Myself, I write. My hand holds the pen and dips it into the ink; and traces it on the paper. When this sheath of mine was very young and was training for my use, it was taught to write, and one part of the sheath learned to take the pen in a particular way, to hold it in a particular way; and always when the "I" wanted to write it was to do this duty, without which the mind, the "I", could not write on the material plane. The "I" might think as much as it liked. It could not produce the material result so that other people might see it and use it, without the help of the sheath. Without this it would be unprovided with any instrument on the lowest plane of the Universe, and so could not work. Atmâ *plus* Manas would be helpless down here unless this sheath can be made into an instrument and taught to produce on its own plane, under orders, what was wanted here for the work. So it was taught and had to learn its lesson, but note this: that when it has once learned it, it continues to do it in the same way, and if I want to change the way of writing, the holding of my pen in the hand, I have got to take a lot of trouble to change the automatic activity of the cells of the sheath, which are independent of my consciousness; when once I have moulded it to my purpose it does what I taught it to do, and it goes on doing it, and if I want to change it, if I mean to change it, I must set to work by repeated efforts, repeated volitions, and I must undo with much pains that which I with much pains before impressed upon the sheath, and I must set it going along the new line, the new direction, that I impose. You see then the automatic action of the sheath, and you see how the sheath has a life of its own, and that this may help or hinder the life which is expressed through it by the "I." If your sheath is to be a help and not a hindrance, if your sheath is to serve you and to be useful to you, you must be its master not its servant, you must be its ruler not its slave. For it is a Karma that you have made; this Karma is the method of automatic action by the body, and it limits you when you want to express yourselves; you have to work within the Karmic limitations that you have made. You are there; you can change them, you can alter them, you can subdue them to the new will that you impose; but you have got to do it step by step, you have got to do it by toil and by effort. Law is Law in every region of the Universe, and you cannot escape its working in the body-sheath any more than anywhere else in the realm of life.

There is a link which I can only just allude to, by which co-ordinated action takes place in the food-sheath; you know what are called the nerves; you know what are called the nervous centres; you know the pillar of nerve matter that goes down the centre of the backbone from the nervous matter of the brain, the threads of nerve matter that go out to every part of the body, and the double nature of the nervous system, one part under the immediate control of the will and the other, automatically acting, carrying on life processes; these, indeed are largely the result of the past action of the will, which has made this vehicle for itelf. Now Prâna acts on these centres, and there is the co-ordinating power, there is the force that is going to make the sheath the vehicle of the "I," and not merely a combination of a number of independent cells and molecules. Not in the sheath of food but in the sheath of Prâna lies the co-ordinating energy, and the food-sheath supplies the nervous centres on which Prâna acts directly as the co-ordinating and controlling energy, so that it may make the food-sheath obedient, and fashion it for the purposes which the higher intelligence demands. But remember this outside sheath is wanted for contact, is necessary to collect experience. Remember it is only a receiver. As a sheath it does not feel. Does that seem strange? When you say a blow struck you, you feel. Do you think you feel at the spot where the blow touches you? Western Science tells you that it is not so. Even Science says that the centres of sensation are in the brain, and we know that if we break the bridge of nervous matter, we may burn the living flesh and no feeling of pain is experienced. Feeling is not in the food-sheath; not in the cells of the body lies the power of feeling pleasure and pain. It only receives the contact and transmits it inwards by Prâna. It has its own feeling in the cells, but *you* do not share that. True, sense-organs are not the senses; true, sight and the eye must be distinguished; true, feeling and the skin and the nerves must be separated; but the sheath has its own feeling. There are certain "massive" feelings, as they are technically called—general fatigue and so on—that are dull sensations of the separate cells transmitting up to the brain what they feel, and coming vaguely into the consciousness of man; not acute, not sharp, not keen, but massive and vague and general; that is the consciousness of the cells; that goes through part of the sheath, passes on as a vague statement of the cells to the consciousness which is within the sheath, which moulds it and controls. And this activity of the cells is the activity of the Atmâ in the matter of the body. This activity in the cells is the Atmâ working in the atoms, working in the molecules, working in the cells. That is the place so to speak—it is a wrong phrase, but I can use no other—the place of Atmâ as regards these individual cells of the body; not working in the sheath as a whole but in every constituent part; for Brahman is omnipresent, all-pervading, as the salt in the water, and can be absent from no spot in space.

Next we come to Prâna, the sheath of Prâna, Prânamayakosha. Now here from the *Kaushitakopanishad* we can find what Prâna really is. It is the outgoing energy of Atmâ. Indra—and the name Indra designates, as you know, the Lord of the atmosphere and the Lord of all the lower world—Indra says—

> I am Prâna,...Prâna is life.*

That is the exoteric form, and the separate name is given of the great Head of the Life-hierarchy of the lower world, that great Entity, who is known as the Deva Indra—not an object of worship for those that can go be-

* iii, 2.

yond, not an object of worship for the spiritually enlightened man, but a mighty Deva, working in the lower worlds, distributing as it were the Essence of the ONE through all the forms of the lower life of things. Now Shankara tells us that this Prâna is Kriyashakti—the Shakti of doing and not of knowing—and there is a distinction of enormous importance. This sheath which is the sheath of Prâna is the sheath of activity, not of knowledge, the sheath which is to actively gather everything, and hand it on to the receptacle which lies within. *But it is not the Knower.* It is the outgoing energy of Atmâ for action, not for thought. And this works in what is called astral or ethereal, matter, in the matter that Science calls ether; and by this it works, and brings all parts into connection, and controls the whole of these lower cells that we have been speaking of, co-ordinating them to make up the food-body of man. This subtler sheath, in which Atmâ as Prâna is working, controls and holds together the whole of the lower matter as sheath. There could be no sheath of food, no physical body, if it were not for Prâna, which co-ordinates all the separated cells and makes them into one complex and orderly whole. That is the function of this Prânic sheath. Prâna works in the subtler matter, in what we sometimes call an astral body. It is not that which in Indian literature is called by this name, the subtle body that we know as Sûkshma Sharîra. Do not confuse them together. Nor is it the Linga Sharîra of the Hindû books, though called by its name. This is an awkwardness of nomenclature that we must keep clear in our minds. It is the lower astral, an essential part of the Sthûlopâdhi and not of the Sûkshmopâdhi. That is necessary to remember, for the astral body that you read of in Theosophical works is nothing more than the Prânic sheath. It is the form-side of Prânic activity, without which Prâna could not act, that is, without which the outgoing energy of Atmâ would not be able to co-ordinate the physical molecules of the external body. We are told in the same *Kaushitakopanishad* that speech, sight, hearing and everything else are dependent on Prâna in the body. Sight is not the eye; Hearing is not the ear; Taste is not the tongue; Smell is not the nose; Touch is not the skin. It is the Prâna in every case which gives the sense-activity to the organs, and which is the transmitter of the outer vibration to the sense-centres which lie in Kâma, in the sheath which is next to that of Prâna, the Manomaya-kosha.

Now understanding that, the next point is that Prâna divides itself into five Prânas, "five-fold dividing itself" says the Scripture, in order that it may uphold and support every part of the body, carry on every vital activity, carry on every function of the body, carry on everything which is necessary for the maintenance of the physical life of the body; and Prâna five-fold dividing itself becomes the five Prânas that are familiar to every one of you. But remember that five is exoteric, and seven is the esoteric number of Prânas, and in the *Mundakopanishad* and in the *Prashnopanishad* Prâna divides itself into seven not only into five. Five for the outer world, because we are now in the Fifth Race, because we have at present five senses, and only five Prânas are in manifestation. But there is a sixth that is going to evolve its sense, and a seventh that must be formed ere yet Man is perfect. And so it is true that Prâna is five-fold in Man in manifestation to-day although seven-fold in its essence ; and that is why in both the Upanishads just named you will find the seven-fold flame of Prâna, not explained but only mentioned, as though to remind every one with intuition that there is a mystery that lies behind, and that the five-fold that is given to the world is not the whole of the Prânic activity, either in Man or the Universe. And then we learn another great truth. It is written :

> From Atmâ this Prâna is born.*

Atmâ is Prâna, and Prânais only Atmâ in activity. Realize that great truth. I quote the words of the Scripture repeating them again, translating word for word :

> From Atmâ this Prâna is born.

It is the outgoing energy of Atmâ. It is the energy of the body. Atmâ in Itself cannot work. I repeat it, because, of the enormous importance that the thought shall be clear. Atmâ in Itself cannot work. It is Sat, quiescent, immovable, un changeable. The outgoing energy is Prâna : therefore it is written that from Atmâ Prâna is born.

Science tells us in its own way something of the same strange story ; tells us how in every part of the world and

* *Prashnopanishad*, iii., 3.

of the body electric currents work. It proves this by the use of the delicate apparatus it invents that it may observe more minutely than by the unassisted senses. Take your brain. Whenever there is thought, electric currents are running through it, and if you test the brain, the instrument answers to the current, and the tiny needle gives a sweep which shows the passage of the current, and proves physically that this electrical action is there. You find the same all over the body, in the contracting muscle and so on. You find electric currents in every part of the body where any functional activity is being carried on. Use your instrument and electricity shows itself, and electricity is only a Western word for one form of Prânic activity. Science further tells you that wherever electricity is there is ether, and without ether electricity cannot manifest. I translate this into the older phrases : wherever Prâna is there also is Akâsha, and without Akâsha Prâna cannot show itself. Thus Prâna is the organiser and controller of the Annamayakosha of man, holding together the complicated aggregation.

Man's constitution should now be becoming a little clearer as to its constituent parts, and the study of life explains "death." For what will death be? It will be the drawing away of this outgoing energy of Atmâ from the sheath of the physical body. It does not, of course, take away Atmâ from the cells of the body, but it takes away Atmâ as Prâna, as the co-ordinating energy of the sheath. The cells of the body break away from each other ; each cell acts in its own way, shows its own life, its own activity, but there is no longer co-ordinated action. In the corpse you find the hairs growing, for instance; then there is life; yet it is not life in the sheath of the body, but it is life in the constituent cells, which are no longer controlled by the Prânamayakosha of man. Think that out at leisure and you will see how these sheaths are going to be used, and how we shall be able to work out their object and their utility, when the whole of them are understood and grasped. We have now got hold of two sheaths, the sheath of food and the sheath of Prâna; the food-sheath that receives from the outer world, the Prâna-sheath which transmits, that outgoing energy which controls and co-ordinates, keeps the body together and subordinates it to the "I" that is going gradually to be built up, the self-conscious intelligence of man. You find that Prâna is the great transmitter, transmitting outwards the moving energy, gathering and transmitting inwards all the contacts from the outer Universe; gathering them inwards always, and therefore a bridge between all the sheaths of man. For this Prânic activity plays through every sheath, and gathering from the outermost carries inwards to the innermost. The *Kaushitakopanishad* tells us that when death comes Prâna gathers everything together, and withdrawing from the body hands everything onwards to the Knower, that is the receptacle of all.*

Now these two sheaths that we have dealt with this morning form together the lowest Upâdhi of Atmâ. These two Koshas together form what we know as the

*iii, 3, 4.

Sthûlopâdhi. If you ask me why I draw your attention to that, my answer is this: that while there are five sheaths, there are only three Upâdhis, and that in Yoga, in practical knowledge, consciousness is going to work separately in each Upâdhi.* There are only three Upâdhis in which consciousness, in which Atmâ, can work, and the highest Adept can separate only these three Upâdhis and cannot separate the constituents of man any further. Râja Yoga is, as you know, the way in which this is learned. Râja Yoga teaches us how we may separate the three Upâdhis one from the other, and how thus may be visited the three regions of the Universe, the sensuous, the intellectual and the spiritual. The three Upâdhis are correlated to these regions, while the sheaths are correlated to the separate Prakritis, to the different kinds of Matter. And H. P. Blavatsky in this connection has said that to whatever nationality the Yogî may belong—whether he be Hindû or Buddhist or Mahommedan or anything else in his outer faith it makes no difference—before he can become an Adept, a Mahâtmâ, a Rishi, he must go through the school of Râja Yoga, and learn this lesson without which Adeptship is impossible. Do not forget that that is true. On this side of the Himâlayas or the other, there is but one school of Râja Yoga, only one and none other, the Eastern School. From time immemorial it has existed, to time immemorial it will stretch, unchanged and immutable, one and the same. The Vedas came forth through it to the Aryan Race, every great Rishi belongs

* See *Secret Doctrine*, vol. i, pp. 181, 182.

to it, and to-day none may rise to the heights of Adeptship unless he pass through that School. Here there may be no confusion as to different schools, no quarrelling as to Eastern and Western, and all the rest of these follies that divide the external world. H. P. B. says, the Messenger of the great Teachers proclaimed, that there is no Adept known to the Great Lodge save Those who learned in and passed through the Râja Yoga School, and studied there; nowhere else may they learn the separation of the Upâdhis, and the conquest of the Universe by knowing that last word of the Science of the Soul.

And therefore it is that I am trying to make you understand—though fettered by the necessary brevity which time-limit puts upon me—I am trying to make you see how all these truths are linked and how while the sheaths I dealt with must be understood, the Upâdhis must not be left out; for without a knowledge of them no practical Occultism is possible, although theoretical Occultism may be understood.

Here I leave it for this morning, taking to-morrow the next two sheaths in which the Self is enwrapped, the sheaths which feel and which are the receptacle, the sheaths which are to hold experience, where building of the individual goes on, and where self-consciousness is gradually evolved.

THE BODY OF FEELING.

If we take the division of man which is used by Manu,* we shall find that that division, though varying in its names, is practically identical with that to which we referred as the division of the Râja Yoga School, that of the three upâdhis as distinguished from that of the five sheaths or koshas. The two sheaths referred to yesterday are sometimes classed together, and are classed together by Manu, as making the Bhûtâtman or elemental self, that is the self which is acting, for he so defines it. He speaks of it as the self which acts, the corporeal self, as it is translated sometimes into English. The main point, to which I want to draw your attention in passing, is that these two sheaths, with which we yesterday dealt, are the two sheaths of action and are related essentially to the elements; are related to the external Universe in those regions familiar to us as the regions of the elements. And in leaving these aside now we pass in a very real sense from the external to the internal world; we pass in a very real sense from the world that we regard as made up of vibrations atomic and molecular to the world

* xii, 12, 13, 14.

which essentially consists in the recognition by the SELF, the translations through the sheath employed by the SELF, of those external vibrations and contacts, into what we will for a moment call sensations and ideas. That is we pass from a world in which the things external to the man are going on, to a world which to the man is internal, and in which everything he considers is no longer a looking outward and receiving from the outside, but a dealing with that which he has received, the manipulating, the elaboration, the working upon materials, by the forces which come to him from the innermost life of all. And so we pass from that body which Manu speaks of as the body of action to the one which he speaks of as the body of feeling. You may remember that he gives it the name Jîva, which is a little unusual, and you may require to read the commentary with it in order to avoid possible confusion; because the way in which Manu uses the word Jîva is not that which connects it with Prâna as Prâna. He defines it as that body in which the Knower, the Kshetragna, becomes sensible of pleasures and of pains. It is essentially this body in which the Knower becomes conscious of pleasures and of pains that we have to deal with to-day.

In their external relations the two sheaths that comprise it, especially the lower of these sheaths, the Manomaya-kosha, are related to the Deva world. I want that point to be very clearly grasped. If you turn to the *Aiterey-opanishad*, you will find that after the Devas were formed, the animals were formed and also man. You may remember that the Devas refused to be satisfied with the animals, but when man appeared they said : "This is good," and entered into him. Now that entering in of the Devas is further described as the entering in of the presiding deities of the elements, and those presiding deities of the elements give rise to sensations in man, receiving from the different elements their suitable vibrations and performing the work of changing the contacts from without into what are called sensations, or the recognition of the contacts, from within. This is essentially a Deva action. This is essentially the work which is done in the making and building of, in the evolution of, the Manomayakosha. It has in it those Devas that belong to the elemental kingdoms. Here comes the link of man with all those lower Devas, the link which, when supreme control has been obtained, makes man the master in every region of the Universe. For the great Adept H imself would be unable to manipulate the lower worlds of matter, the lower worlds of sensation, if it were not that He possesses these sheaths co-ordinated into perfect harmony and perfect subordination, and which none the less connect him with the external Universe ; inasmuch as these belong to the Devas, he, having the Devas subject to him, has subject to him also every region of the external Universe that they control. Great then is the importance of this sheath, and the two together which we have to consider are the most important sheaths of the whole. This Manomayakosha is the one that we will take first, and in that we shall find we have got together the elements which will make the basis of the individual Self-consciousness which gradually is to be evolved—not Self-consciousness, but the materials on which consciousness is going to work and which, ideally reflected into itself, will make the true individual Self-consciousness possible. How difficult and how complicated the subject is, you will realise even from this suggestion. I can only hope that in putting it to you I may give—probably to those who have not studied it for themselves—not a complete idea but the materials, so to speak, on which you may afterwards yourselves work, and so out of the materials make up for yourself a completer and fuller realisation.

Now, for a moment I must ask you to think of the animal world ; because in the animal world we get, not the Manomayakosha, but some of the elements that enter into it, that which is really only the germ of the higher ; that in which and by means of which, the higher will later be developed. And just as I asked you yesterday to realise the internal changes of the atoms, by which the atoms become differentiated from within, and built through the mineral, vegetable and animal kingdoms, gain a peculiar additional capability and increasing complexity which enable them to form more elaborate combinations, so in dealing with these sheaths, which are connected in the lower part with the animal kingdom, I must ask you to realise the changes that occur in connection with what we know as feeling in animals. That which only exists in the germ, not in the vegetable but in the animal kingdom, is developed, and becomes what we know as the human power of sensation, the higher feelings of pleasure and of pain. Not that man is evolved from the animal as such—that is the Western blunder—but that the materials which go to build the Manomayakosha in man have been evolved in the animal kingdom, and these materials carry on the results of their evolution, and are therefore available for the building of man. You notice the point of difference : it is not that man is directly evolved from the brute, as Darwin teaches ; it is that the materials which have been elaborated in the animal kingdom are then used for the building of Man. Quite a different thing from the purely physical succession, and introducing a different idea ; this may show you what underlies and forms the strength of the Darwinian theory, for it is the truth that gives it the strength, although there is also the blunder which comes from studying from without instead of from within, by looking at everything from the standpoint of the external pole of Matter instead of from the internal pole of Spirit.

Now let me, having guarded myself for the sake of clearness of conception, see what we have in the animal kingdom of this power of sensating pleasures and pains. We notice in animals what we have spoken of as desire : that is an outward-going attraction towards objects that are external, so that when contact is experienced what is called pleasure is felt. We notice also that this outward-going energy comes into contact sometimes with objects which do not by contact give pleasure but pain, and we then notice that repulsion is the result. Attraction by contact, which inwardly is translated into pleasure. Repulsion from contact, which inwardly is translated into pain. Not that pleasure and pain are in the external object, but that contact between the outer and inner is either a contact of harmony and, therefore, is pleasure to the feeler, or is a contact of discord and by the feeler is translated as pain. That is really the essence which underlies these words. Vibrations meet each other; some are harmonious—Pleasure; some are discordant—Pain.

But pleasure and pain cannot exist either in one set of vibrations alone or in the other. They exist in the contact between the two. Leave those vibrations outside and they are harmonious in themselves; there is neither pleasure nor pain, but there is, motion. Take the inner; there also there are vibrations; but these are not pleasurable nor painful. They are in, and in connection only with, the Knower. But when the two come into contact, and come against each other, they are either harmonious or discordant; then by contact arises pleasure or pain, which is harmony or discord at the point of contact of the vibrations. That, if you think it out, will enable you to realise how it is possible to overcome pleasure or pain, and how the vibrations from outside may continue and may be realised in thought—after experience has been gained—while by the severing of absolute contact it will no longer be the discord or harmony which we know as pleasure or pain reflected on the inner sheath.

Now in the animal there is this to notice ere we leave

it. That pleasure and pain in animals are very brief. There may be a feeling of pain arising from a discordant contact, say a blow, but it is brief. An animal, say with a broken leg from a fall will, when the agony of the contact is over, turn and eat food. It will eat and enjoy—provided it has not come much into contact with man. That is a strange point to keep in your minds and which needs to be explained. The wild animal, evolved along the line of nature uninterfered with by the consciousness of man, does not suffer in the same sense as the domesticated animal suffers. Its pleasure and pain are very brief, its pleasure and pain have not the same element of continuity. The wild animal, which falling has injured itself, is even found eating calmly with a broken limb. It is a strange fact to notice, and a fact which throws much light on the evolution of the inner consciousness. But that is not all ; the animal does go one step further, but very very very slowly. Realise that it takes the step, because otherwise you will be forgetting that in Atmâ is every possibility. Although It be involved in all these lower stages, It is there enfolding all possibilities, It is there enfolding all potentialities ; and in the lower animals we find the germ, as it were, which when we come to deal with the further elaboration of these materials in the human being, we find developed into the possibility of thought. And what is the essence ? It is a connection between the outer object and the inner sensation, and the recognition of this connection, the recognition that the two things are joined together, that when one occurs the other will follow—this is the beginning of thought, making the link between the outer object and the inner sensation. Very very very slowly is that made, and very imperfectly in the lower animals. Let me give you one instance to show exactly what this means, an experiment. There was a fish, a pike, kept in a large glass-case of water. In the West they are very fond of keeping animals to look at, and there are aquariums in which water-creatures are preserved, so that they may be studied and kept under view. In one of these there was a fish, a pike, and between the place where the pike was and the next box of water there was the glass wall, of course invisible. This fish naturally going onwards as animals will and pursuing fish in the adjoining compartment constantly struck its nose against the glass which it could not see. Over and over and over again that went on. Week after week, month after month; no connection recognised between the blow and anything external, no link of thought, until at last the repetition of this vibration, coming from without and felt as shock, formed a dull link between that particular spot and the impossibility of going forward, and the fish turned before it touched the glass. Then the glass was taken away; but to the pike the impossibility of going forward remained, and it invariably turned when it reached that place where the glass had been, having slowly made the connection between external object and internal sensation, which is the germ of thought. This connection between the external object and the internal sensation persisted after the object was removed, because the thought-power was germinal, because the thought-power was not elaborated ; so when the external object was removed the connection ideally remained, and the creature turned when nothing stopped it, merely because there was in the pike the beginning of thought without the power of being able to carry it further and adapt it to the varying conditions. Now supposing that you realise that, you will understand what is meant by instinct. It means the tendency to repeat continually that which has been felt. To repeat it unconsciously, as we say, that is without previous volition and distinct recognition. The instinct of animals is in that stage, corresponding to the automatic action of the lower sheaths of which I spoke. Presently we shall find we have : automatic action, then instinct, then we shall find memory, unconscious almost or partial, then gradually active, then complete. For this is all part of the great law of Rhythm which works in every region of the universe. Now I can leave my animal. I was obliged to make this digression ; it was necessary in order that you might realise the complicated nature of what we mean by the Manomayakosha. I was obliged to show you how in the animal kingdom the response to pleasure and pain has been evolved. In order that man might be builded it was necessary that the materials of the sheath should be ready to be co-ordinated together.

And next we shall also perceive that there is a limit to the upward working of Atmâ from the lowest stage of the physical, that there is a point where no further progress is possible unless there is the co-operation of another factor evolved in a past Universe, in a past Manvantara. All evolution is not only a becoming for the present, but also the preparation for a future Manvantara. All evolution, as we shall see in a moment, is carried on by co-operation. From the results of the past there is going to be a further process of becoming, which in its turn will help in the next Universe that is evolved. For thus we shall begin to realise what we are doing and what we evolve, how we are being helped by the evolution of the past and how we shall help in the evolution of the future. And by " past" I mean a past Universe, and by " future" I mean a future Universe, separated from this by Pralaya, separated from us by a long period of repose, but linked to us by that unbroken law of Karma which is of the Essence of the Supreme and is, like It, without beginning and without end. Co-operation, I say, is wanted. And how? Now there is going to be evolved what we call Mind—the power of thought. It must be evolved by the co-operation of the minds that have been evolved and perfected in a previous Universe. Take the *Aitereyopanishad* again: you will remember there is something more than the entering in of the Devas. Paramâtmâ said: " How shall I enter in?" There is to be something more than these sheaths which are made as it were along the primary line of evolution. Now we must seek the minds that have been already evolved, the Sons of Mind we call them. We have now to come to the building of Man, the making possible of a new humanity.

And now I must turn for a moment to my Western

Science and give you a microscope to help in the understanding of this next stage. Suppose you take a germ developed in, we will say, a plant—it does not matter a bit whether we take a plant, an animal or man, for the purpose of my argument—a germ-cell in a plant, say a flower; pulling the flower to pieces, throw aside the calyx and the petals, which are simply protective; throw aside the male organs, for we do not need them yet; and going into the very centre, the very middle of the flower, we find there a sheath, and when we open this sheath little bodies like seeds. When we open these little bodies, we then want to help our eyes with some magnifying power, that we may see further and thus examine these bodies, or ovules. I find a cell within the ovule, a cell that is called the germinal cell. And going further still within that even I find the nucleus, as it is called; and then still further the nucleolus. Is it not strange that in Modern Science we are doing exactly the same as Uddâlaka did when he taught his son and made him take a seed and open case after case to find the germ of the future tree within the seed; Uddâlaka did it just for the same purpose that I am turning it to this morning, that we may understand the power of Brahman the invisible, and that within the seed there lay enfolded the future material tree. But I am doing this by way of Science, so we are quite respectable. Within my tiny germ what do I find? Possibility. But one side of possibility only and not the whole. For if that germ be left to itself nothing more will happen. Everything has been done that can be done by the female side to make the germ ready for future growth and the development of a new individual. But the individual is not there: only the preparation. The female side of Nature can do nothing but prepare the receptacle, wherein shall be assembled together everything that is necessary for the nourishing of the future individual, but something more is wanted ere further evolution can take place. Within that germ there are possibilities, but there is as yet no individual. For the making of that new individual there needs the junction of two forces and not the growth of one alone. And although the germ be there, and the tracing of the future, there is no possibility of growth unless from outside some new force shall arise. How does it come? It comes from that which I threw aside in my first dissection of the flower; from those male organs which for the moment I did not require. And from these there comes the force enwrapped in the form which is the other side of the dual evolution with which we are now familiar—the invigorating, the vitalising, the fertilising energy, which by itself can do nothing, which by itself is sterile, as that other also is barren; but which coming to the other, meeting the other, will give rise to a new individual. That is the point that I want you to grasp. For mind you, there is one Law and one Life everywhere, and that which in material nature you can see with your eyes, you can see with your mind in the higher regions of the Universe. For Brahman is one and His works everywhere show the same nature, and the sameness is felt through the difference of the materials. The principle of evolution is the same everywhere, for Brahman alone is the energising force, and His Nature is the Law by which everything is evolved. When this union has taken place, then only growth begins; when this union has occurred, then only a new individual is slowly and gradually formed. *The beginning of the individual* is at the point of junction; although the essence be eternal, the junction is a point in time; where the junction occurs, there is the beginning of the individual as individual, although the essence of which he is formed is eternal, undying, and knows neither ending nor beginning.

Now we have the materials to enable us to understand the coming of the Sons of Mind, evolved in a past Manvantara by the processes that we are undergoing in the present. And the coming of these Sons of Mind to the helping, as it were, of the lower nature is exactly parallel to the coming from the stamen of the invigorating energy which shall vitalise the germ within the seed and give birth to the new individual. And so in those wonderful stanzas that come to us from the far side of the Himâlayas, in those ancient, most ancient, stanzas, it is written:

FROM THEIR OWN RUPA THEY FILLED THE KAMA.*

From Their own Rûpa They filled the receptacle which had been slowly prepared for the filling:

SOME PROJECTED A SPARK.*

That spark is as it were the plasm of mind; coming from those in whom mind had been evolved in a pre-

---

* *Secret Doctrine*, vol. ii, p. 20.

vious Manvantara, and filling with its energising and vitalising force what I will call the female germ in the receptacle of which we have been speaking, it gives the possibility of a new individual, a Self-consciousness, an Ego, an Ego to be slowly evolved, but none the less taking its start from the union which now is accomplished. For the spark projected from the Flame of Mind is to fire the material upon which it has fallen, and from that a new Flame will arise, identical in its essence with that which generated it, but separated in its individuality for purposes of manifestation. And this is why it is said that you may light a thousand candles from a single flame, and the flame is never diminished, although a thousand flames are visible where only one was visible before.

Now we shall be able to understand, I hope, our Manomayakosha. For what now will occur? You have now the beginning of the sheath which is able not only to receive contact from without, but, by this impulse which has been thrown into it by the generating Mind, will become able to complete the power of connecting the outer object and the internal sensation, of which we saw the unfolding possibility in the animal but which is the characteristic of the mind in man. And this recognition of the connection, this understanding and taking into consciousness in an ideal form of the constant link between the external object and the inner feeling is the beginning of the working of mind in man, and is the peculiar function of the sheath with which we are concerned. For by feeling—the power, that is, of answering to the impressions from without—it gains those contacts through the outer sheaths which are necessary in order that Self-consciousness may be made gradually possible and then, having translated the outer contact into sensation—that is the first stage—it transforms the sensation into the idea; that is, it changes it by a process of elaboration; it changes the contact which gave rise to the sensation into an ideal form, which it then preserves as material. These ideal forms are what we call percepts technically, or the thoughts that are to be the material on which the Knower is to work, elaborating them into concepts, and building up gradually the individual that is Self-conscious and is to be ultimately all-knowing. The Manomayakosha, then, collects all these sensations and turns them into percepts, that is the connection between the outer object and the internal sensation; and then elaborates the percepts into concepts, that is, changes the recognition of the connection into the ideal form which is capable of preservation and is the material for all possibility of future thought. And this is in truth the process of thinking. The internal image, as it is technically called, is the ideal form of the sensation which has been rendered possible by the contact that I have explained; and the work of the Manomayakosha is to do this elaboration. It is just like the crucible of the chemist into which he throws different materials and a new combination comes out—not new in its essential elements, but new in its combined existence. He puts them in, but working on each other they bring about a combination which is the outcome of the interaction between them, not of the separate action of each. You must realise that just as there is a difference between the threads of cotton separate and the cloth into which those threads of cotton are woven, so there is a difference between the separated sensations and the elaborated ideas woven out of them by the mind, or, if we take our chemical illustration, which are gradually elaborated in the crucible by the interaction of the forces of attraction and repulsion. When that is accomplished the beginning of Self-consciousness is present.

Consciousness is everywhere; how shall we distinguish it? It is so hard, because we only know Self-consciousness, and are not sufficiently advanced to take from each sheath its own material in the state of elaboration brought about by the sheath, and study the result. But dimly, I think, I can put it to you. Consciousness may be taken as the response of a gradually separating centre to that which is around it—the mere response; Self-consciousness is when in addition to the response there is the recognition of the "I" that responds. Not the response only, but the knowledge of the response; not the response only, but the recognition of the response. For the "I" is builded by the memory that links all these percepts and concepts together, and so really gives that continuing consciousness which makes the recognition of an "I" as apart from that which is "not-I."

Now let me take still a step further. It is said in the *Mundakopanishad:*

The organ of thinking of every creature is pervaded by the senses.*

This emphasises the double action of Manomaya-kosha. It is in truth the organ of thinking, but is also pervaded by the senses; that is, you have this double action going on in it always, the receipt from without and the elaboration from within. And that is why this sheath is so difficult to understand; that is why so much depends on the understanding; that is why you cannot master it until you begin to understand. And that is why knowledge is necessary if the SELF would become free and know Itself as Itself alone. For here is the element of confusion, here the element of contact, here the function from without and from within, and hence the strongly illusory "I" that I shall want to deal with more fully when we come to-morrow to speak of the use and control of this sheath. For the moment I must leave it with that great statement of the *Mundakopanishad:*

The organ of thinking is pervaded by the senses; that organ purified, Atmâ manifests Itself.

We shall see why that is when we deal with the purified organ and the changes that result.

Now at death there is a separation in this sheath; all the lower Deva element passes from it; all the Deva element, which joins man to the world of Devas becomes separated from the next sheath, and from the Manomaya-kosha. For here is the rending that is caused by death, and this part waits, as the Devas wait in Devaloka, to

* iii, 9.

bring the SELF back to earth and bind it to the necessity of rebirth. There lie the chains, there lie the bonds, there the links of desire which keep the SELF imprisoned and tie it to the wheel of births and of deaths. When death occurs every particle is set free, but the links remain to bind It, until by Its own deliberate action they are cut.

But I must take the other sheath, which is very easy to understand and grasp; the real subtle difficulties lie in the understanding of the one that we now for the moment leave. I take the discriminating sheath, that which is called the Vignânamayakosha—the particle "Vi" implying the discriminating, separating and arranging of things—the Vignânamayakosha which is to be the sheath of the SELF by which the lower sheaths are to be mastered. Into that sheath experiences are reflected from the Manomayakosha as ideal concepts; into it is reflected everything which in the Manomayakosha is collected. The one is the collector and elaborator, the other is going to arrange and to discriminate, to have the whole of this elaborated collection as material to work on, the whole of this as material by which it is going to gain higher consciousness and a more perfect cognition of the individual SELF. For what is the process of Atmâ in this sheath? It works on the internal images, it works on those ideal and elaborated forms reflected into it from the other sheaths; it works on them and elaborates them further, and it has its special work, what we call abstract reasoning of the loftiest kind; no longer sensations, no longer perceptions, no longer the making of ideas, or the elaboration of ideas, but the discriminating between them, then the arranging of them, and then the reasoning from them. So that the special work in this sheath is the work of abstract reasoning, dealing with pure ideas, separated from the concrete presentations, the realm of truth, no longer so illusory as the other. For here we have the abstract and not the concrete, the pure internal working no longer confused by the senses, nor in any way interfered with by the outer world; there is pure intelligence, clear vision, intelligence unmoved by the senses, intelligence tranquil, strong, serene. That sheath must be realised, that sheath must be understood, for there lies the creative power of meditation, there lie all the energies that grow out of one-pointed contemplation. There is the creative sheath of man, as in the Kosmos Divine Ideation is the creative sheath whence all comes forth; for just as in the first lecture I reminded you that in the divine form of Shrî Krishna as shown to Arjuna, the divine eye when given to Arjuna saw all forms of living things which in the Universe could exist, so in this sheath of man, in ideal reality, there exist all forms that can come forth, to which objective reality may be given by this creative power. That is the force of Atmâ in the sheath with which I am dealing, for the outgoing energy of Atmâ in this Vignânamayakosha is the force which dominates and moulds everything that is external to it, from which the creative energy of Atmâ can work through the lower sheaths when they are purified.

We can now take another problem, so easy once we

have reached this point that one wonders why it was so confusing and difficult before we reached it. That with which we have to deal are Will and Desire. What is Desire? Desire is the outgoing energy of Atmâ, working in the Manomayakosha, and attracted by external objects. That is, Desire is outward-going energy attracted from without, and its direction governed from without. What is Will? Will is the outgoing energy of Atmâ working in this Vignânamayakosha, and dealing no longer with choice directed from without but with choice initiated from within, moulded on the internal images by a process of discriminative reflection. So that the outgoing energy is guided from within in its direction, whereas in Desire it is attracted from without. The direction in one case comes from the external object, in the other from the inner Life that chooses and wills. Hence what you call strong and weak will in men. What is weak will in man? A man with a weak will is the man that is always drawn by desire towards external objects that attract him and he goes after them. He is weak in will. Why? Because he does not rule himself, choosing his road by the power of memory, reason, judgment, and discrimination, and everything that should make him steady in the midst of a moving Universe. He is drawn out by the external object and goes out after everything that attracts him by a desire for contact, and he goes as circumstances attract him. If he be surrounded by temptations, if he see something pleasant, he desires to obtain it, if he see beauty he desires to enjoy it; so he is at the mercy of external circumstances, and we say that the man is weak and we never know what he is going to do. But the strong-willed man is the man who having gathered together all these experiences and having translated them into ideal forms, compares them and arranges them, and discriminating between them and understanding the connection between pleasure and pain, and understanding the sequence which sometimes makes a momentary pleasure the womb of a future pain, he, knowing all this and remembering, chooses from the inner standpoint; and the outer circumstances may be exactly what they like, the inner man stands unmoved and chooses as he knows.

Here I find I must leave the subject for this morning. In truth these two sheaths are completed, as far as in so brief a space I may complete them. And I need only in closing say this morning that this inner man passes from birth to birth, carries on his memory life after life. These ideal forms persist in the sheath; these ideal forms brought out of one life are carried on into another, and so are continually growing, until the highly evolved Ego begins to be master of the lower sheaths, and the creative force that resides within comes forth, and he is no longer guided from without. For the process of evolution leads to the controlling of the lower by the higher, the less differentiated by the more highly evolved. So that in this sheath sovereignty shall at last be centred, and all shall be obedient to the impulse of the One within; coming back to birth, it picks up the lower Deva-elements it left for a while, and it has to bring them back time after time until they are absolutely subject to its will. It contains all the essence of all experiences. It contain the very inner quality of everything through which it has passed on earth.

Now you will see why it is written that as the wind passes through a garden of flowers and does not pick the flowers, but takes the fragrance from them and goes on fragrance-laden, so also Atmâ passing over the garden of experience gathers, not the facts, sensations and phenomena, but as it were the fragrance, the ideal form of each, and goes on with all this aroma of experience fragrance-laden into the bosom of its God.

THE OBJECT OF THE SHEATHS.

BROTHERS :—We have studied during the last three mornings the question of Atmâ manifesting through certain sheaths, and we have dwelt at some length and with some care on the two outer sheaths whose special work is that of collection; then with the two inner sheaths whose special work is that of elaborating that which has been collected from without and transmitting the results, and that of assimilating that which has been collected and transmitted. To-day we have to deal with the last of the sheaths, and then I purpose to sketch for you, very imperfectly, the method of the working and the use of the sheaths, so that we may thus complete our subject and have it—however rough and poor in its outline, yet that outline complete—and then by further study for ourselves and above all by further meditation we may succeed in filling in the details that are lacking and come to a real understanding of the whole. Now the great difficulty that lies before us this morning in trying to gain any idea at all of the nature of Anandamayakosha is that a state of consciousness which has not been experienced by a person is a state which that person is unable to conceive or to understand. There are many states of consciousness in the Universe as various as the various kinds of living things—and all is life. Professor Huxley, for instance, dealing with this difficulty, has pointed out, that there is nothing contrary to the analogy of nature in conceiving that there are states of consciousness higher than ours; that as there are many lower than the human, so there may be many states of consciousness that rise above that which we speak of as the human, that there may range above us, stage after stage, grade after grade, consciousness after consciousness, becoming loftier and loftier, greater and greater, wider and wider in limits, consciousness ever expanding, until it is possible to imagine, although not to understand, the consciousness that shall include everything that exists; and then he (Professor Huxley) points out that such a consciousness would be as much higher than ours as the human consciousness would be incomprehensible say to the consciousness of a black-beetle—and we may add, as incomprehensible to us in its workings as ours to the black-beetle. This is a thing necessary to realize; otherwise we limit everything by our own limitations, and fall into the error of imagining that because we cannot conceive therefore that which to us is inconceivable has no existence in fact. Try to realize, for instance, how incapable we are of understanding a lower state of consciousness. That of a creeper, as example, which spreading over a wall sends out tiny tendrils and pushes a tendril into a hole in the wall in order that it may grasp it and find support in the roughness within;

and then withdraws the tendril finding the hole unsuitable, and travels over the surface of the wall until it finds another and testing the other finds that perchance suitable to its needs. How can we translate in thought the consciousness of that vegetable creeper? How can we realize in our consciousness—so different—what is the impulse that makes it follow its path, that makes it go into a particular hole, enables it to know that it is unsuitable, and to search for another which is suitable wherein it remains? What dim, vague and strange consciousness is it which thus communicates what is necessary for the growth of the plant, and yet shows us nothing that we realize as consciousness in action, in feeling, in anything that we can identify with our own? And then conceive again for a moment—for I want you to realize this, ere I put what I know will be so difficult even to sense—try and think what it would be if some lower animal, some insect or fish or quadruped, seeing a philosopher sitting in abstract contemplation, trying to deal with some mighty intellectual problem, insensitive to outer impressions, concentrated within the realm of mind, if that lower creature tried to understand the working of the mental consciousness of the philosopher, and to judge whether he was wise in his method, whether he was wasting his time or no. You can realize how foolish would be the attempt; you can realize how incompetent would be the judgment. Try then for a moment to realize that there may be above you more than there is below you, a condition of consciousness as much mightier than that you know in the brain, as yours is mightier than the consciousness of the plant, of the insect, of the fish or of the quadruped; and then, not so much thinking but if you will, trying to sense and to feel, follow consciousness inwards and feel that which cannot be translated into words, try and sense a possibility, where Atmâ, clad but in the Anandamayakosha, begins in that last sheath to come face to face with Itself which is Brahman, that sheath making a delicate film of separation which still will preserve the duality necessary for the recognition, and at the same time being so thin, so delicate, and so subtle, that it seems wellnigh as though the Knower and the known were one. The one sheath remains, for without a sheath no manifestation. Without a sheath there would be unity, and then all thought as we know it ceases, our form of consciousness is impossible. Brahman cannot act without the sheath of the Universe that He makes for himself. Brahman cannot act in manifestation without the sheath which makes manifestation possible. Having, as it were, centred all life and energy within the last sheath, the sheath of bliss—Anandamayakosha—then let us listen for a moment to the sacred words which give some glimpse of the glory, and may lead us into some dim sense of that which lies beyond the veil; it is written:

> He, all-wise, all-knowing, glorious in the world, in the divine town of Brahman, placed in the ether, standeth Atmâ; of the nature of mind, ruler of Prâna, of the body, of food. Concentrated in the heart, by the knowledge of THAT, the wise behold the Radiant, whose body is bliss, immortal.*

* *Mundakopanishad*, ii, II, 7.

There are moments, supreme and rare moments, that come to the life of the pure and the spiritual when every sheath is still and harmonious, when the senses are tranquil, quiet, insensitive, when the mind is serene, calm, and unchanging ; when fixed in meditation the whole being is steady and nothing that is without may avail to disturb ; when love has permeated every fibre ; when devotion has illuminated, so that the whole nature is translucent ; there is a Silence, and in the silence there is a sudden change ; no words may tell it, no syllables may utter it, but the change is there. All limitations have fallen away. Every limit of every kind has vanished ; as stars swing in boundless space, the Self is in limitless Life, and knows no limit and realizes no bounds : light in wisdom, consciousness of perfect light that knows no shadow, and therefore knows not itself as light ; when the thinker has become the Knower; when all reason has vanished and wisdom takes its place; who shall say what it is save that it is bliss ? Who shall try to utter that which is unutterable in mortal speech—but it is true and it exists. That is the Anandamaya-kosha where the Atmâ knows Itself ; its nature is bliss ; all the spheres have ceased ;* all else has gone ; none but the pure may reach it ; none but the devotee may know it ; none but the wise may enter into it ; for, once again, it is said that :—

Steadfastly by truth, by austerity, by perfect wisdom, by Brahmacharya-practice, is this Atmâ attained. In the midst of

* *Mândukyopanishad, 12.*

the body, clad in light. He whom the sinless and subdued behold is pure. *

It is Brahman. It is the Logos of the Soul. It is the Atmâ conscious of Itself. But on that the fewest words the best, and though I may not leave the stage unspoken of, I leave it quickly, because to reach it there must be yearning to aspire ; because truth, wisdom, devotion and purity are asked for the vision, and this must be won by many a struggle, ere the Pure shall see the Pure. We are told that it is bliss. The end of pain is bliss. Here, there is struggle and agony and friction, but at the end is bliss and bliss unspeakable. So that in all the trial of life, and in all the anguish and misery that may overwhelm the soul of man, in the struggle that leads it wellnigh to despair, those, who once have known, know for evermore, and in the worst of agony the centre in the heart is calm, for it knows that the end shall be in peace and that harmony shall be the close of strife. Let us, thus realizing, come to regions where our foot is surer, regions more fitted for your feet and mine, that still are in the mire of earth and that must learn to tread the path of which the end is bliss unutterable.

Let us now come back to a lowlier study, having caught a glimpse from a mountain top as it were, of a land that lies beyond, into valleys of earth where our lot is cast, and let us realize how that end shall be gained, the path that leads to it and the methods that

* *Mundakopanishad,* iii, I, 5.

shall guide us towards it; for while it may be well for a moment to realize the goal, it is still more important to find the road that leads to it and to begin, not in mere hope and yearning, mighty as those are, not only in aspiration and in desire, to achieve it here, in the life that we lead here, in the place in which we learn how we may set our feet on the Path and by knowledge wedded with devotion may find our way at last. So, I come to the working of the sheaths. Before I conclude with their use I want you to see the working, because by the realization of the way in which they work, we shall solve so many of the problems that puzzle us every day, problems that hinder our growth, problems that are, as it were, like fetters which prevent us from walking freely, which make things so difficult to understand, that we grow discouraged and sometimes fall back into lack of belief, unable to grasp the belief which it is so difficult to understand. The first result of the working of Atmâ in these many sheaths is the setting up of a number of illusory "I's," apparently conscious entities, and we find in ourselves when we look inwards, a struggle, a conflict and a war, as though we consisted of many "I's" instead of one, many Egos instead of one Ego. Self-consciousness must be a unit; none the less we are confused by this apparent multiplicity, and these "I's" that yet are not the "I," are a constant source of disturbance, of mental confusion, and of moral mistake. Let us then try and understand what they are, and how they come to be. Let us see how far they are illusory, and what it is that makes them seem real. For mind you, the conflict to us is real enough whether the combatants are illusory or are not.

We understand that Atmâ is working in all the sheaths. We have conceived, taking sheath by sheath, something of the nature of, and the working in, each; and it is very easy to realize that if we stand outside and look at them from without, we shall not see the one worker but the moving sheath, and that the moving sheath as different from another moving sheath will at once give an apparent individuality, an apparent separation, and therefore place for conflict. If, for instance, looking from without, I see the body which is at work, and then I trace the activity of Prâna, and then I see the passions carrying a man away, and then see the mind interfering and pulling him back again—studying like that from without I see all these different things warring the one against the other, because I am looking from the side of differentiated objects and not from a centre where the unity of action might be perceived; and just as you may go into a room full of machinery and see many whirling wheels, and see many apparently independent bars swinging from side to side, as the Engineer might take you and show you the one point at which all the force was generated and from which the whole was moved and controlled: so by wisdom may we place ourselves in the centre, and see the one outgoing energy which is differentiated in the sheath and not in Itself, so that the actor is really one, although that in which it is acting gives this apparent diversity. But there is more. That is not a full explanation. Take the body: not only have we learned that the atoms and molecules and the cells of the body have their independent life, and are living as atom, as molecule, as cell, but we have also learned that they are co-ordinated into the food sheath, they act *as a sheath.* That is they act together under the co-ordinated energy ; they act, ruled by the common life, as sheath ; and we have further learned that thus acting, there is what we call automatism produced. That is to say, when a sheath has acted along a particular line over and over and over again, that then its inherent energy—which is also of course Atmâ but Atmâ *in the sheath*—its inherent energy tends to reproduce, without the direction of the central consciousness, the actions which it has continually practised ; so that automatic action is set up in which the central Self-consciousness takes no longer any active part. Two things cause this : first the habit of repetition of that which is caused originally by purposive action. I pointed out to you that when you learned to write, it was by deliberate effort, by well-concentrated endeavour ; that a child's hand is trained to write and traces, line after line, all the words that it desires to form. The Thinker is working there and moulding the child's hand to its own purpose as an instrument. When it is taught and trained, it can do it over and over and over again without conscious effort ; then the sheath takes up the work and repeats the accustomed motions ; it is continuing automatically what was a purposive action at the beginning ; automatic action repeats that to which the body has heen trained, and if you want to change it, you must bring the will to bear on the change; otherwise repetition is the law of the sheath's action, the great law of rhythm, the universal law everywhere working of a tendency to repeat; the night and the day! the light and the darkness! the ebb and flow of the ocean; all the revolutions of moon, of sun, of stars—all regularly rhythmically repeated. That is the law of the Great Breath, and everything is dominated by it, whether it be atom or central sun in space. Therefore it of course rules the sheath of the body, the food sheath; and this tendency to repeat what once has been impressed upon it, is the law of rhythm working in a particular sheath, and repeating without the active consciousness of the Ego, all actions repeatedly imposed upon it previously by that purposive will. So, again you get in the third sheath inwards what we call "instinct." I need not work that out similarly in detail. It is automatic action plus feeling; but it is exactly on the same lines. Acts which have been done over and over and over again are repeated unconsciously as we see. Coming on then still further, you find the beginning of the third "I," partly conscious of itself, because it remembers partially. That is the brain consciousness which has memory, although a fragmentary one, of the life during which it has been working. You get in every one of us this brain consciousness of the "I" which is based on a partial memory, that is the memory of the life during which it has been the organ of the Thinker. And then there is the real "I", whose consciousness is able to stretch back to every life behind it, and that contains as receptacle every experience that in myriads of lives has been gathered. Thus all these "I's" are there, and only one is the real "I," but when a sheath reflects its illusory "I" on to the real one, then the real "I" lends its own self-consciousness to the reflection thrown on to it by the sheath, and so you have this apparent reality which is illusory, and is lent by the one consciousness, which transfers to that which it looks on as separate its own individuality, and gives to the reflection within itself the apparent and deceptive reality of life. So, might you take an image in a mirror for the real man. If a mirror is so placed that it does not show itself as a mirror, say, at the end of a passage, you may think that the reflections that are there are objects that lie further on, and that you will find as external objects as you advance; thus every sheath reflects on to the consciousness its own image and to this self-consciousness is erroneously attributed by the Ego that receives them all.

Now you will find that a light is thrown on our limitations, our individual Karma, by this view. See how the self-conscious Ego must be limited by the working of the sheaths; see how that which in the past it has done, and which comes back to it as the automatic action of the body and the astral, which comes back to it in the Manomayakosha, as feelings, as motions, as instincts, every one which it has gathered in its pilgrimage through many lives; how all these must govern, limit and control it, when it comes into these sheaths for any particular life. You cannot separate one life from another. You cannot deal with human lives as though they were separate individuals, for they are not. The life that you are in now is to the Ego but as a day. Death is as the night which closes it. Birth comes with the dawning, and that is as another day of life. And the next death is as the night in which you lie down to slumber. Can you separate to-day from to-morrow? Can you get rid to-morrow of all the obligations that you have entered into to-day? Will the night get rid of them and set you free from them? or, are you held crippled and controlled by them, and have to work them out bit by bit, piece by piece, not freely, because you have bound yourselves, and because one day is conditioned by the days that have gone before. So with lives. These lives are days, and these deaths are nights, and they are bound one to another, and the Sutrâtmâ, the Thread-Soul, passes through them all. Thus you begin to see why you are bound. You begin to realize the reality of the Karma that limits you; but in recognizing the limitation, forget not the freedom. In recognizing the sheath that limits you, forget not the Atmâ that permeates the sheath, and moulds it in the permeating. *You* are Atmâ, "Thou art That." Thou, being Brahman, art never crippled so as to be unable to move. There is the paradox of at once our slavery and our freedom. Bound by the doings of our past, but remaining Brahman in the centre, that knows no limit and that is moved by Its own Nature alone. When then will harmony come out of the conflict? Clearly when they all are subordinated to the One Life, and when everything comes from the vibration from within. There is the end of strife. When the SELF has permeated and dominated everything, and in the higher sheaths has gained Self-consciousness, and gradually Self-consciousness on every plane, then inasmuch as all the vibrations will come from within, and none outside will have power of spreading disturbance, then there will be perfect harmony and co-ordination between sheath and sheath. That is why the true Yogî knows no disturbance. That is why the true Yogî is ever harmonious and serene. Though the sheaths are there, no outer vibration may avail to make disturbance; though the sheaths are there, they will not answer to anything that comes from without. They know their Master. They recognise the hand that holds them. They are like the well-broken horses of a chariot, answering only to the hand of the driver, which no longer is rigid but light and easy as the hand of a child. Then there is perfect harmony and peace and bliss.

We have to study the use of the sheaths, our last point. Why all this conflict and work? Why all these many sheaths, and these myriads of lives, and these millenniums of years? Why these countless successions of lives and deaths? Why this endless procession as it were of the days and nights of Brahmâ? Why all these? Let us see if we cannot understand. Let us see now if, with the knowledge that we have been trying to gather together, we cannot understand something of the purpose of the Universe, something of the outcome which makes it worth while that a Universe should be. We have seen that there is the gathering of knowledge. But to what purpose? for mere gathering is not sufficient. The gathering of knowledge by each sheath is for this pur pose: namely, that the kn owledge may remain for use, while that which is its material shall be powerless for disturbance. We have seen that the o uside Universe show s itself to our senses by way of v ibration, and that these vibrations shake the sheath. We have seen further that w hile knowledge is gained by these vibrations in the sheath that thus answers to the vibrations from without, in the progress and the growth of the Ego, the Individual, all this knowledge becomes reflected in an ideal form, and is finally realized by the Ego not as affecting itself but as having been gathered for the purpose of use. The whole process of development consists in this; that you learn to touch, that you learn to feel, that you learn to know, and then gathering that up, you possess the whole of it for utility, while it has lost its power to disturb you and so to fetter you to the acts that you perform. Easily I think in a few phrases can I show you the steps of this growth. Cast your mind back to that point of junction that I spoke of yesterday, where the baby Ego, so to speak, was born by the joining of the two lives. That Ego knows nothing of the world into which it has come, literally a baby Soul, unconscious of law, ignorant of everything that surrounds it. There is only in it desire, outward-going energy. It goes out, attracted. Sometimes it enjoys. It goes out again. Sometimes it suffers. It shrinks back. On and on it goes like this, through the whole of the life, aye, through many lives, and after a considerable time, it begins, as I hinted to you yesterday, to make the connecting link between the sensation of pleasure or of pain and the outer object, and that is the first thought; that thought being a perception, *i.e.*, the connexion that joins together the object and the sensation, and so makes the material on which reasoning may be possible. Thus gradually going on, the baby Ego begins to gather experience, and learns that there is law. The result of all this feeling of pleasure and pain, and of joining together the pleasures and pains with outer objects, of the reasoning upon them, all this teaches this child-Ego growing out from babyhood to childhood—teaches it that it is in a world of law, and that wherever there is pain it has struck itself against the law; teaches it that only by obedience to the law can it avoid pain and find the harmony that is pleasure. Many hundreds of lives are needed to learn this perfectly; many hundreds of lives, as we count lives—to the SELF, they are but one. During each of these, lessons are learned. Just as in the present human life we went to school, and just as we passed from class to class as we learned more and more and became worthy to go higher, and from school to college and from college into the outer life of the world, so it is with this Ego, this Individual, that is growing in many lives, passes from one life to another, passes from one stage to another; then gathering knowledge in each life it comes back wiser than it was before, until it gains its manhood and has something of the knowledge of the world in which it is to live and work; and then it gains something more. Using the sheaths in this way, it kills out desire by experience; for, it learns that although there are many desires that being in harmony with law give pleasure, that none the less, they sometimes turn into wombs of pain, by the great law that is impressed on all that is not Brahman as Reality, the Law of Change, the Law of Weariness. You enjoy a legitimate enjoyment, and you get tired of it. When you have enjoyed it to the full, you are worn out and you get a feeling of disgust and you are weary of it. You eat legitimate food and enjoy, and the appetite is satisfied, and it turns aside from that which attracted it. So with every material satisfaction. You enjoy it, yes; but it cloys. You become satiated and weary. That is the only way of finally getting rid of desire. Desire vanishes when you realize that all desires that are not directed to the Permanent have in them the element of pain. When you find that time after time the joy is followed by weariness, you say: "Of what avail is it to enjoy for a moment and then to be weary? Let me seek joy where joy is permanent, and where the more I have the deeper shall be enjoyment and peace and happiness." For there is this difference between material and spiritual bliss; the one cloys and disgusts, while the other increases with every new consumption. With every increase there is still more increase that lies beyond. That is the difference between the life of the divine and the material, between the life of the inner SELF and the life of these outer sheaths. Never shall desire be dead till that lesson is learned, and the SELF turns inwards to Its own centre, which is infinite, in which bliss can never be exhausted nor lost. And so, the use of the sheaths is not only to gather knowledge, and not only to learn the law of pleasure and pain, but also to get rid of the root of desire, without which there never can be peace and bliss unspeakable.

And then there is the third use which I was going to say is the most important of all. I say it is the most important, because it deals with all men and not with the individual. It deals with humanity and not with the single man. The third use of the sheath is that in the sheath you many feel, and feeling you may learn sympathy, and learning sympathy you may take succour to those who are in pain ; for remember the life of the God is the life of giving. Do you remember what Shrî Krishna said? That there was nothing He need do. He acts, not for Himself, but because if He did not, the whole world would stop. There then is a higher teaching still than yet we have reached. The use of the sheaths is that we may learn sympathy by suffering, and knowing what it is to be in anguish may carry help to our fellow, who has not learnt the lesson. We feel in the sheath. How shall we sympathise? Sympathy is only perfect when pain is felt in the sheath, vibrating to every throb of agony from the outside world, but when the SELF knows Itself as separate from the sheath, and realizes the pain, feels it *in the sheath*, but is not disturbed in Itself by the vibration that is agonising the sheath in which It is clothed. Try to follow the thought. It is possible to feel pain with the uttermost anguish. It is possible to feel the whole of your outer world throbbing with agony and with anguish that needs your whole will to master it. It is possible that the Manomayakosha shall be full of pain and every fibre strained almost to the breaking point, and yet that the Self within, knowing the pain and feeling it by reflection, and entirely conscious of every throb of agony, is yet absolutely still, calm and unshaken. No pain touches It, though the pain is felt in the sheath, and It can act with perfect steadiness, with perfect wisdom, unblinded by the pain and unshaken by the anguish, and therefore absolutely at human service with every expanding energy and with every force that It possesses. There is the triumph.

When man by myriad lives has reached a certain point, when man by myriads lives has reached the entrance of what is technically called the Path, then the Guru comes forward to take that man in hand, to lead him along the Path of discipleship and give him the final lessons in the understanding of the sheaths and of the SELF; and then along that Path, with the Guru, Who guides him, he goes for still a few more lives learning these final lessons, and having learned them, and being there within the sheaths, and yet in a strange kind of fashion, separated, then there comes at last the point where the Soul, the individualised Self, absolutely free from all desires and yet dwelling within the sheaths, stands where It may go onwards into freedom, or turn backwards to help the world. If it wills, It has a right to go onward, onward into bliss, onward into All-consciousness, onward, having conquered all the regions of the Universe, into the One, the unlimited, the All. Or it may, if It wills, turn back: not again to be in bonds, not again to be fettered, not again that desire shall grip It and tie It to birth and death ; but by a voluntary choice, by a self-made decision It says : "I will not have final peace till my brothers share It ; I will not have final liberty that is not shared by my brothers, and enjoyment which is not theirs. I will not take Nirvâna for myself and leave my brothers in the bonds of birth and death, in their ignorance and in their darkness, in their helplessness and in their folly. If I have won wisdom, I have won it for their enlightening. If I have won strength, I have won it for their service. If I have learned to vibrate in agony for man, what avail is it then to throw aside the sheaths and go on where no agony is useful? I will stay where I am and will work for man. Every pain of man shall strike me. Every agony of man shall touch me, and shall wring my heart. Every folly of man shall be my folly by identification with humanity, and every sin and crime of theirs my suffering until the whole of us are free." Such is what we call the Master. Such is the Mahâtmâ of the Hindû, the Arhat of the Buddhist, the Supreme and the liberated SELF that remains voluntarily within the sheaths as long as Its brethren are in bondage and puts Itself at human service by the supreme act of renunciation, to remain in bondage till the whole are free, and to go into Nirvâna when all can go hand in hand with Him.

There is the purpose of the sheaths; there is the sublime triumph; there is the glorious ending. When the Manvantara is over, there shall be myriads of individuals as the results of that Manvantara, and at their head, these triumphant Ones who have led them onward, have taken them onward into rest, into Nirvâna, of which no words may speak, to the Place of Peace and Rest and All-consciousness, that is in store for humanity. And then on the other side Those who have triumphed bring back Their memory, Their individuality, and Their knowledge, to the building of a new Universe, to the making of a new race. They are the Sons of Mind that I spoke of yesterday, Who came to the help of the world, so that the baby-Egos might be formed and the new individuals might start. Thus do the Mahâtmâs of the past Manvantara come back, as it were, as Gods for the building of the worlds. That is the possibility for all who choose the whole instead of the individual, who choose love instead of selfishness, and service instead of gain. We must begin it to-day. We must begin it in our lives, in duty to wife, to child, to nation, to humanity. Never is a great One made save where the smaller duties are first accomplished, and that which in the end is a Mahâtmâ, at the beginning was a self-sacrificing Grihastha in the home.

A CATALOGUE

OF BOOKS

FOR SALE BY

THE THEOSOPHICAL PUBLISHING SOCIETY

7 & 8 DUKE ST., ADELPHI, LONDON, W.C.

1895

A CATALOGUE OF BOOKS

ÆSCH MEZAREPH, or Purifying Fire. Collected from the *Kabalah Denudata* of Knorr von Rosenroth. Preface, Notes and Explanations by Sapere Aude. Cloth, 8vo. 2s. 6d.

In any other form than the present, this important and valuable work is virtually unprocurable. It will interest all students of occultism, and may be regarded as furnishing one of the most important keys, for the true interpretation of the Hebrew Scriptures.

AN ADVENTURE AMONG THE ROSICRUCIANS. By F. Hartmann, M.D. An account of a dream-visit to a Rosicrucian Monastery, and of the topics expounded by its Adept inmates. Cloth, 12mo. 5s.

ANNIE BESANT.—An Autobiography. Illustrated. Cloth, 8vo. (pub. 6s.) post free 4s. 10½d.

APOCRYPHAL NEW TESTAMENT.—Being all the Gospels, Epistles, and other pieces now extant, attributed in the first four centuries to Jesus Christ, his apostles and their companions, and not included in the New Testament by its compilers 3s. 6d.

ASTRAL LIGHT, THE. An attempted Exposition of certain Occult Principles in Nature, with some remarks on Modern Spiritualism. By Nizida. Cloth, 8vo. 2s. 6d.

ASTRAL PLANE, THE. Its Scenery, Inhabitants, and Phenomena. By C. W. Leadbeater, *Sec., London Lodge, T.S.* pp. 94. 1s.

ASTROLOGY.—Astrology; a series of Lectures delivered before the Mylapur Literary Society, Madras. By Walter R. Old. Wrappers, 8vo. 1s. 6d.

ATLANTIS, The Antediluvian World. By Ignatius Donnelly. Cloth, 8vo. 9s.

AZOTH, or The Star in the East. By Arthur Edward Waite. Imp. 8vo. cloth. Cheaper edition. 5s. 6d.

The conclusions reached in this work are the result of considerable research into the significance of the Hermetic and Mystical Symbolisms contained in alchemical literature, and, as regards fundamental doctrine, they offer a reasonable harmony between the transcendental teachings of Eastern and Western Theosophy.

BHAGAVAD GITA. Translated by Annie Besant. Pocket size, whole morocca or calf, 4s. Cloth 2s.

Do. Do. Cheap edition on thin paper, and paper covers. 6d.

BHAGAVAD GITA. The Great Indian Epic, with an introduction by W. Q. Judge. Leather, 15mo. 4s.

BHAGVAT GITA, THE., or Dialogues of Krishna and Arjun. Translated by Charles Wilkins. Cloth, 12mo. 4s. 6d.

BHAGAVAD GITA, DISCOURSES ON THE. By T. Subha Row. 3s.

BHAGAVAD GITA, THOUGHTS ON. By a Brahmin F.T.S. Boards, 8vo. 2s.

BLOSSOM AND THE FRUIT, THE. The True Story of a Black Magician, a Tale of Mystery and Adventure. By Mabel Collins. Boards. 2s.

BUDDHISM.—Buddhist Catechism, A; according to the Sinhalese canon. By Col. H. S. Olcott. 1s. net.

BUILDING OF THE KOSMOS, and other Lectures. By Annie Besant. 2s. net.

"Sound; Fire; Yoga; and Symbolism are the subjects treated of in this most excellent book. The essay upon Yoga, the Kingly Science of the Soul whereby a man may attain to that Divine Wisdom which is his birthright, deserves to be read of all men. To lovers of the Scriptures of the World the essay on 'Symbolism' will appeal strongly and will be found most helpful, for in those Ancient Writings the most important truths are frequently veiled from the superficial reader by an allegory or a symbol, and in this essay the reader will find a clue to the method by which the study of symbols may be approached with beneficial results. Considerable light is thrown upon some of the very complex symbols pertaining to Indian Philosophies."

BURIED ALIVE. An examination into the Occult causes of apparent death, trance, and catalepsy. By Franz Hartmann, M.D. (Contains chapters on "Reported Cases of Premature Burial"; "The Philosophy of Death"; "The Signs of Death"; and "The Prevention of Being Buried Alive." 3s. 6d.

CAVES AND JUNGLES OF HINDUSTAN, FROM THE. By H. P. Blavatsky. Cloth, 8vo. 7s. 6d.

"A delightful and fascinating book. Madame Blavatsky saw many things that would have escaped the notice of an ordinary observer, and the reader is alternately startled by the deep knowledge she proves herself to possess of the almost unknown religions of India, and moved to admiration at the perfect knowledge of the world."—*East London Advertiser.*

CHALDEAN AND ZOROASTRIAN ORACLES. 2s. 6d.

CHRONOLOGY OF ANCIENT NATIONS, THE. An English Version of the Arabic Text of Al Biruni, with Notes by Dr. C. Edward Sachau. Imp. 8vo. Pp. xvi. and 464 (pub. at £2 2s.). Cloth. 10s. net.
"A book of extraordinary erudition, compiled in A.D. 1000. To all who seek to trace the remains of ancient nations it is indispensable."

CHUANG-TZU, Mystic, Moralist, and Social Reformer. Translated from the Chinese by Herbert A. Giles. Imp. 8vo, cloth. 16s.
"Full of noble and lofty teaching. Should be in everyone's library."

COMING RACE, THE. By Lord Lytton. Cloth. 1s. 6d.

CORY'S ANCIENT FRAGMENTS of the Phœnician, Carthaginian, Babylonian, Egyptian and other authors. By E. Richmond Hodges. Cloth, 8vo. 7s. 6d.

CYCLOPÆDIA OF INDIA AND OF EASTERN AND SOUTHERN ASIA, THE. By Surgeon-General Edward Balfour. Third edition. 3 vols. Cloth, 8vo (pub. at £5 5s.). 30s. net.
"There is no other work in the English language in which is brought together an equal amount of information on everything connected with India."

DEATH—AND AFTER? By Annie Besant. Prettily bound in cloth. 1s.
"A popular exposition of *post-mortem* states, according to the Esoteric Philosophy, now known as Theosophy."

DESATIR, THE, or the Sacred Writings of the Ancient Persian Prophets. Together with the Commentary of the Fifth Sasan. Boards, 8vo. 3s. 6d. net.

DIVINE PYMANDER OF HERMES. Translated by Dr. Everard. Preface by Dr. W. Wynn Westcott. Cloth, 8vo. 3s. net.
"One of the few fragments preserved to us of the Esoteric Wisdom of Ancient Egypt."

DREAM OF RAVAN, THE. A Mystery. Cloth 8vo. 2s. 6d. net.
"It is beyond question that the unknown writer of this work was both a scholar and a mystic. That he had studied the *Râmâyana* from the original texts and was a master of Vedântic psychology is amply manifested; that he was a mystic himself and spoke of things that were realities to him and not mere empty speculations is evident to every earnest student of Indian theosophical literature.

In no other western publication have the three 'states' of man's consciousness been so strikingly and so intelligibly set forth as by our author. This mystic exposition will endow such intellectual productions as Professor Max Muller's *Lectures on the Vedânta* and Doctor Paul Deussen's *Das System des Vedânta* with a soul, and breathe into them the breath of life. In this work the mystic and student of yoga will recognise many a home truth but slightly veiled, and many an important secret wholly disclosed."

ECHOES FROM THE ORIENT. By Wm. Q. Judge. Cloth. 2s. 6d.

ELIXIR OF LIFE, THE. From a Chela's Diary. By G—— M—— F.T.S. Wrappers. 1s.

ESOTERIC BUDDHISM. By A. P. Sinnett. Cloth, 8vo. 3s. 6d.

ESOTERIC BASIS OF CHRISTIANITY, THE. By W. Kingsland. Cloth, 8vo. 3s. 6d.

FIVE YEARS OF THEOSOPHY. Being Selected Articles from the first five volumes of *The Theosophist*. Second and revised edition. With a Glossary and Copious Index. Cloth, 8vo. 10s. net.

GEMS FROM THE EAST. A Theosophical Birthday Book. Compiled by H. P. B. Beautifully embellished with Sketches and Symbols of the Orient. Parchment, 12mo. 3s. 6d.

GHEBERS OF HEBRON, THE. By S. F. Dunlop. Cloth, 8vo, pp. 1006. 21s.

"A monument of indefatigable research."

GLEANINGS FROM INDIAN CLASSICS.—Heroines of Ind. Cloth, 8vo. 2s. 6d.

"Interesting as illustrating the status of woman in Ancient India."

GLEANINGS FROM INDIAN CLASSICS.—Tales of Ind. Edited by Mamnatha Natt Dutt, M.A. Cloth, 8vo. 2s. 6d.

"Selected from the famous Indian Classics."

GOLDEN STAIRS, THE. Tales from Wonder World. By Arthur Edward Waite. Cloth 8vo. 2s. 6d.

The lessons these stories are intended to convey are unmistakable, but not so obtrusive as to weary even those of tender years, and so charming is the language in which the stories are told, so picturesque the scenes presented, that many children will turn to these pages again and again with delight.

GUIDE TO THEOSOPHY, A. Containing selected Articles for the Instruction of Aspirants to the Knowledge of Theosophy. Boards, 8vo. 5s. 6d. net.

GREEN LEAVES. By Mabel Collins. 1s.

HERMETIC ARCANUM OF PENES NOS UNDA TAGI. Preface and notes by Sapere Aude, Fra. R.R. et A.C. Cloth, 8vo. 2s. 6d.

HOLYROOD, A MIDNIGHT VISIT TO. By the Countess of Caithness. Cloth. 5s.

HOMEWARD. Songs by the Way. By A. E. Wrappers. 1s. 6d.
"A volume of mystical poems of great beauty."

HOURS WITH THE MYSTICS. By R. A. Vaughan. Cloth, 8vo, 2 vols. 12s.

H. P. B.—In Memory of Helena Petrovna Blavatsky. By some of her Pupils. Wrappers. 1s.

IAMBLICHUS ON THE MYSTERIES OF THE EGYPTIANS, CHALDEANS, etc. Translated from the Original Greek by Thomas Taylor. 7s. 6d.

Iamblichus on the Mysteries is one of the most important of the translations from the Greek which were executed by the industrious and ingenious Thomas Taylor, the modern disciple of Plato and the ancient Greek Philosophers. It forms a manual of the ideas of the ancients upon the great questions of religion and philosophy, on which, indeed, it forms one of the most elaborate and detailed expositions which have descended to us.

IDYLL OF THE WHITE LOTUS. By Mabel Collins, Wrappers, 8vo. 2s. 6d.

INCIDENTS IN THE LIFE OF MADAME BLAVATSKY. By A. P. Sinnett. With portrait, cloth, 8vo. 10s. 6d.

INDIAN PALMISTRY. By Mrs. J. B. Dale. Cloth, 8vo. 1s.

IN THE PRONAOS OF THE TEMPLE OF WISDOM, being the History of the True and the False Rosicrucians. By Franz Hartmann, M.D. Cloth, 8vo. 7s. 6d.

"Probably the best and most reliable of recent books on the Rosicrucians. The Author, whose great work, *The Secret Symbols of the Rosicrucians*, is so well-known to Hermetic Students, here gives a brief history of the Rosicrucians and treats at some length of the chief tenets of the Order; of the present work he says, "the doctrines presented herein contain the most profound secrets."

ISIS UNVEILED. A Master Key to the Mysteries of Ancient and Modern Science and Theology. By H. P. Blavatsky. Royal 8vo, about pp. 1,500, 2 vols. £2 2s.

A marvellous book both in matter and manner of treatment. Some idea may be formed of the rarity and extent of its contents when the index alone comprises fifty pages, and we venture nothing in saying that such an index of subjects was never before compiled by any human being.

JEHOSUA, The Life of the Prophet of Nazareth. By Franz Hartmann, M.D. Cloth, 8vo. 7s. 6d.

KABALISTIC ASTROLOGY. By Sepharial. 2s. 6d.

KEY TO THEOSOPHY. By H. P. Blavatsky. Being a clear exposition in the form of question and answer of the Ethics, Science and Philosophy, for the study of which the Theosophical Society was founded. Cloth, small 4to. 6s.

LETTERS THAT HAVE HELPED ME. Compiled by Jasper Niemand. (Reprinted from *The Path.*) 2s. 6d.

LIGHT ON THE PATH. A Treatise written for the personal use of those who are ignorant of the Eastern Wisdom, and who desire to enter within its influence, written down by M. C., Fellow of the Theosophical Society. New edition, with notes by the Author. Fcap 8vo, cloth. 1s. net.

MAN, Fragments of Forgotten History. By two Chelas in the Theosophical Society. Contents: Preliminary; Supra-Mundane Man; Physical Evolution of Man, or Descent into Matter; Primitive Man; Evolution of Sex; The Fourth Race—Atlanteans; Early Aryans; Growth of Language and Religion; Man and other Orders of Existence; The Occult Hierarchy. Cloth, 8vo. 4s.

MANDUKYA UPANISHAD WITH GAUDAPÂDU'S KÂRIKÂS AND THE BHÂSHYA OF SANKARA. Translated by Manilal N. Dvivedi. 4s. 6d.

MESMERISM, The Rationale of. By A. P. Sinnett. Cloth 8vo. 3s. 6d.

MODERN SPIRITUALISM. A. P. Sinnett. 1s.

MONISM OR ADVAITISM? An Introduction to the Advaita Philosophy, read by the light of Modern Science. Comparison of the conclusions of the Aryan Advaita with those of the Monistic Philosophy of Europe and America. By Prof. M. N. Dvivedi. Wrappers, 8vo, pp. 144. 4s. 6d.

MYSTERY OF THE AGES, contained in the Secret Doctrine of all Religions. By the Countess of Caithness. Cloth, 8vo. 8s. 6d.

MYSTIC QUEST, THE. A Tale of Two Incarnations. By W. Kingsland. 3s. 6d.

NATURE'S FINER FORCES. The Science of Breath and the Philosophy of the Tattvas. Translated from the Sanskrit, with introductory and explanatory Essays on Nature's Finer Forces. By Râma Prasâd, M.A., F.T.S. Cloth, 8vo. 4s. 6d.

"A learned treatise on the occult forces in the cosmos and in man."

NEW ASPECTS OF LIFE AND RELIGION. By Henry Pratt, M.D. Cloth, 8vo. (Published 7s. 6d.) 3s.

"Among other works, we would recommend especially to students of theoretical Occultism, *New Aspects of Life and Religion*, by Henry Pratt, M.D. It is full of esoteric dogmas and philosophy." H. P. Blavatsky, in *The Secret Doctrine.*

NIGHTMARE TALES, THE. By H. P. Blavatsky. Wrappers. 1s.
Cloth. 1s. 6d.

"A volume of weird and thrilling stories of magic."

NOTES ON NIRVANA. By G. R. S. Mead. Cloth, 4to. 2s.

"A scholarly work on a subject of great interest.

NUMBERS; Their Occult Power and Mystic Virtue. Being a *resumé* of the Views of the Kabbalists, Pythagoreans, Chaldean Magi, and Adepts of India. By W. Wynn Westcott. Cloth, small 4to. 4s.

"The only work now in print that is entirely devoted to the Magic of Numbers. The subject is one in which the Great Mystics of all ages have ever taken a vivid interest, and to which nearly all have contributed something of their occult learning, and in this volume is collected together much of their teaching, from Pythagoras to H. P. Blavatsky, from Plotinus to Paracelsus."

OCCULT SCIENCE IN INDIA AND AMONG THE ANCIENTS, with an account of their Mystic Initiations. By Louis Jacolliot. Cloth, demy 8vo. 12s. 6d.

OCCULT WORLD. A. P. Sinnett. 3s. 6d.

OCCULT SCIENCE IN MEDICINE. By Franz Hartmann, M.D. Cloth, 8vo. 3s. 6d

"Treats a subject of vital interest to all with great ability."

OCEAN OF THEOSOPHY. By Wm. Q. Judge. Paper. 2s. 6d.

POSTHUMOUS HUMANITY, a Study of Phantoms. By Adolphe D'Assier, Member of the Bordeaux Academy of Sciences. Translated and annotated by Henry S. Olcott, President of the Theosophical Society. Cloth, 8vo. 7s. 6d.

PRABÔDHA CHANDRÔDAYA, or Rise of the Moon of Intellect. And Atma Bodh, or Knowledge of the Self. Boards, 8vo. 2s.

PLOTINUS. By G. R. S. Mead. 1s.

RAMAYANA OF VALMIKI. Translated by Ralph T. H. Griffith. 10s.

REINCARNATION. By Annie Besant. Cloth. 1s.

A popular explanation of Reïncarnation, according to the Esoteric Philosophy, now known as Theosophy. It deals with the wide spread of the Doctrine; what it is that reïncarnates; what it is that does *not* reïncarnate and why we do not remember our past lives; a reply to the question, can human souls transmigrate into animals? the method of reïncarnation; thought forms; the building of character; the object of reïncarnation; the great renunciation; the causes of reïncarnation; what determines successive reïncarnations; the proofs of reïncarnation; recurring cycles in history; rise and decay of races; objections to reïncarnation; the increase of population; the law of heredity; effect of the belief on life.

REINCARNATION, A Study of Forgotten Truth. By E. D. Walker. Comprised in fifteen chapters and an Appendix, giving a Bibliography of Reïncarnation. Cloth, 12mo, 350 pp. 3s. 6d.

REINCARNATION, A Study of the Human Soul. By Jerome A. Anderson, M.D. Wrappers, 8vo. 2s. 6d.

"An excellent book. The best presentment of Reïncarnation from the scientific standpoint that we have yet had."

REMINISCENCES OF H. P. BLAVATSKY AND "THE SECRET DOCTRINE." By the Countess Wachtmeister. Cloth, 8vo. 2s. 6d. Wrappers. 1s. 6d.

ROSICRUCIANS.—Mysteries of the Rosie Cross, or the History of that curious Sect of the Middle Ages known as the Rosicrucians. Parchment, 8vo. 7s. 6d.

ROSICRUCIANS.—The Secret Symbols of the Rosicrucians of the Sixteenth and Seventeenth Centuries; with a Treatise on the Philosopher's Stone. Translated from the German by Franz Hartmann, M.D. The plates of the Secret Symbols, 27 in number, have been coloured by hand, exactly duplicating the originals which Dr. Hartmann secured during his researches among ancient MSS. and Occult Works in Germany. £1 5s.

ROSY MITE, or the Witch's Spell. By V. P. Jelihovsky. Illustrated. Cloth, 8vo. 2s. 6d.

SACRED MYSTERIES AMONG THE MAYAS AND QUICHES, 11,500 years ago; their relation to the Sacred Mysteries of Egypt, Greece, Chaldea and India. Freemasonry in times anterior to the Temple of Solomon. By A. Le Plongeon. Illustrated. Cloth, 8vo. 15s. net.

SANKHYA KARIKA, THE. By Iswara Krishna. Translated by Henry Thomas Colebrook; also the Bháshya, or Commentary of Gaudapáda. Translated by Horace Haymah Wilson, M.A., F.R.S. Boards, 8vo. 4s. 6d. net.

SCIENCE OF ALCHEMY, THE, Spiritual and Material. An Essay by "Sapere Aude." Wrappers, 8vo. 1s. net.

SECRET DOCTRINE, THE. The Synthesis of Science, Religion and Philosophy. By H. P. Blavatsky. Cloth, 2 vols. and Index. £2 5s. net.

"At once remarkable and interesting—remarkable for its wide range of curious and ancient lore, interesting for the light it throws on the religions of the world."—*Pall Mall Gazette.*

SELF AND ITS SHEATHS. By Annie Besant. 1s. 6d.

SEPHER YETZIRAH, the Book of Formation and the Thirty-two Paths of Wisdom. Translated from the Hebrew. By Wm. Wynn Westcott, M.B. Cloth, 8vo. 2s. 6d. net.

This very ancient Rabbinical Treatise is a curious and instructive remnant of the learning of the pre-Christian era, and has always possessed a great fascination for occult students. By the great Rabbinical School of Theosophy and Occult Learning, it was regarded as containing the fundamental principles of the archaic wisdom.

SEVEN PRINCIPLES OF MAN, THE. By Annie Besant. Cloth. 1s.

A popular exposition of the constitution of man, according to the Esoteric Philosophy, popularly known as Theosophy. It deals wirh the physical body and its consciousness; "the double," or ethereal body; the life principle; the passional self, developing after death into the "spook"; thè brain-mind of man; the higher mind; the spiritual soul; the spirit. Also with the phenomena of the séance-room, of mesmeric and hypnotic trance, thought-reading, etc. The appendix gives some details about the Theosophical Society, and a list of Theosophical books and pamphlets suitable for the student.

SHORT ENQUIRY CONCERNING THE HERMETIC ART. By A Lover of Philalethes. Preface by Non Omnis Moriar. An Introduction to Alchemy and Notes, by S. S. D. D. Cloth, 8vo. 2s. 6d. net.

"One of the few really good works on this subject."

SIMON MAGUS, an Essay. By G. R. S. Mead, B.A. Cloth, 4to. 6s. 6d. Paper boards, 5s.

"An important work for students of Theosophy and Gnosticism. In this monograph we have presented to us, in admirable order, all that is to be found in the New Testament, in the Fathers, in the so-called Clementine Literature, and in the Constitutiones Sanctorum Apostalorum relating to Simon Magnus. To the student of Comparative Religion, this work will be of the highest value, and the future writer on early Christianity, who desires to treat his subject fully and fairly, cannot neglect the aspects of the teachings of Simon here presented to us by Mr. Mead."

SOMNIUM SCIPIONIS. Translated into English. With an Essay "The Vision of Scipio" considered as a fragment of the Mysteries. By L. O. The Golden Verses of Pythagoras. By A. E. A. The Symbols of Pythagoras. By S. A. 1 vol., cloth, 8vo. 2s. 6d. net.

"Not since 1804 has any English version of the two famous Pythagorean treatises included in this volume appeared in book form. Of their importance it is sufficient to state that they have been justly held in the highest esteem by Mystics from an early period to the present time. This has also been the case with the *Somnium Scipionis* or Vision of Scipio, Cicero's famous essay. L. O.'s able essay will be found most valuable to students."

STANZAS OF DZYAN, THE (from *The Secret Doctrine*). Translated by H. P. B. ∴ Wrappers. 2s. 6d.

"A very few copies for sale."

STRANGE STORY, A. By Lord Lytton. 1s. 6d.

STUDY OF MAN AND THE WAY TO HEALTH. By J. D. Buck. 325 pp., bound in half Russia. 10s. 6d. net.

"This book should be in the hands of all Theosophists."

THEOSOPHICAL ESSAYS. By Annie Besant. 2s.

THEOSOPHICAL ANALOGIES IN THE "DIVINA COMMEDIA." By L. Schram. 1s.

THEOSOPHY, A GUIDE TO. Containing Selected Articles for the Instruction of Aspirants to the Knowledge of Theosophy. Boards, 8vo. 5s. 6d. net.

THEOSOPHICAL GLOSSARY, A. By H. P. Blavatsky. Cloth, crown 4to, pp. 389. 12s. 6d.

"The above work will be found invaluable by every student of Theosophy and Occultism. Everyone should possess a copy."

THEOSOPHY, RELIGION, AND OCCULT SCIENCE. By Henry S. Olcott, President of the Theosophical Society. With Glossary of Indian Terms and Index. Cloth. 7s. 6d.

THOUGHTS ON BHAGAVAD GITA. By a Brahmin F.T.S. Boards, 8vo. 2s. net.

" Invaluable to the reader of the *Bhagavad Gitâ*."

THROUGH THE GATES OF GOLD. A Fragment of Thought. Contents:—Prologue, The Search for Pleasure, The Mystery of the Threshold, The Initial Effort, The Meaning of Pain, The Secret of Strength. Cloth. 4s. 6d.

TRANSACTIONS OF THE BLAVATSKY LODGE (London). Part I. 1s. 6d.

Has an interesting chapter on Dreams.

TRANSACTIONS OF THE BLAVATSKY LODGE (London). Part II. 1s.

Contains valuable Notes on Astral Light, Elementals, Electricity, Gravity, Genesis of Planets, etc. By H. P. B.

THE TRUE CHURCH OF CHRIST, Exoteric and Esoteric. By J. W. Brodie-Innes. 3s. 6d.

UPANISHADS, THE PRINCIPAL TWELVE. With Notes from the Commentaries of Sankaracharya. Translated into English. Cloth, 8vo, pp. 710. 10s. 6d. net.

UTTARA GITA. Translated by Rai B. K. Laheri. Wrappers, 16mo. 1s.

VASUDEVAMANANA, or the Meditations of Vasudeva. A Compendium of Adwaita Philosophy. Translated from the Sanskrit. Wrappers, 8vo. 1s. 6d. net.

VOICE OF THE SILENCE, THE, being Extracts from the Book of the Golden Precepts. Translated by H. P. Blavatsky. 2s. 6d.

VOICE OF THE SILENCE, THE. Pocket edition, bound in cloth, 2s. In whole calf or morocco. 4s.

WHAT IS THEOSOPHY? By Walter R. Old, with a Preface by Annie Besant. Boards. pp. 128. Post free, 1s. 2d.

WONDER LIGHT, THE, and other Tales for Children. Cloth. 3s.

YOGASARA-SANGRAHA of Vijnana Bhikshu. Translated by Gangânâtha Jha. 2s.

YOGA APHORISMS OF PATANJALI, THE. An interpretation by William Q. Judge, assisted by James Henderson Connelly. With Preface and Appendix. 3s. 6d.

YOGA.—A TREATISE ON THE YOGA PHILOSOPHY. By N. C. Paul. Boards, 8vo. 2s. net.

YOGA.—THE YOGA OF CHRIST: or the Science of the Soul. Written down by A. K. G. Edited by F. Henrietta Müller, B.A. Cloth, 8vo, 2s. net. Wrappers, 1s. net.

"This book appeals especially to that large class of devout souls who find neither satisfying Truth nor edifying practice in modern Christianity: who believe, nevertheless, that Christ had a message for them, and that somewhere hidden beneath the noise of words, and the misinterpretations of sectarians, a Truth, divine and living, may be found."

YOGA PHILOSOPHY. A Compendium of the Raga Yoga Philosophy, comprising the principal Treatises of Sankaracharya and other renowned authors. 3s. 6d. net.

YOGA.—Raja-Yoga (second edition). Translation of the Drgdrsyaviveka of Bhâratitirtha and the Aparoksanubhuti of Sankaracharya, with copious notes to explain the practical bearings of the text, and introduction containing a critical general account of the results of Aryan thought compared with the conclusions of modern science. By Prof. M. N. Dvivedi. Wrapper. 4s. 6d. net.

YOGA-SUTRA. Translation (literal) of the aphorism of Patanjali, with notes critical and explanatory, based on about eight reliable commentaries; introduction explaining the outlines and bearings of the subject, and an Appendix containing extracts from the "Hatha pradipikâ" for practical guidance. By Prof. M. N. Dvivedi. 3s. 6d. net.

YOUR FORCES, AND HOW TO USE THEM (White Cross Library). 6 vols., each complete in itself (to order only). Per vol. 9s. net.

ZANONI. By Lord Lytton. Cloth, 8vo. 1s. 6d.

ZOROASTRIAN AND SOME OTHER ANCIENT SYSTEMS. Compiled by D. J. Medhora, F.T.S. Cloth, 8vo, pp. 308, 12s.

PAMPHLETS.

THE MASTERS AS FACTS AND AS IDEALS. Annie Besant. 6d

THE INDIANAPOLIS LETTERS ON THEOSOPHY. By Alex. Fullerton. 6d.

THE WILKESBARRE LETTERS ON THEOSOPHY. By Alex. Fullerton. 6d.

THE PLACE OF PEACE. By Annie Besant. 3d. and 2d.

THE ESOTERIC BASIS OF CHRISTIANITY.
Part I. By Wm. Kingsland. 4d.
Part II. GENESIS. By Wm. Kingsland. 4d.

WHY I BECAME A THEOSOPHIST. By Annie Besant. 4d., post free, 4½d.

THEOSOPHY MADE EASY. By Major Hand. 3d., post free, 3½d.

WOMANHOOD AND THE BIBLE. By Libra. 3d., post free, 3½d.

THEOSOPHY AND ITS EVIDENCES. By Annie Besant. 3d., post free, 3½d.

THE SPHINX OF THEOSOPHY. By Annie Besant. 3d., post free, 3½d.

THE THEOSOPHICAL SOCIETY AND H. P. B. By Annie Besant. and H. T. Patterson. 3d., post free, 3½d.

A ROUGH OUTLINE OF THEOSOPHY. By Annie Besant. 3d., post free, 3½d.

1875 TO 1891: A FRAGMENT OF AUTOBIOGRAPHY. By Annie Besant. 2d., post free, 2½d.

IN DEFENCE OF THEOSOPHY. A Lecture delivered in St. James' Hall. By Annie Besant. 2d., post free, 2½d.

THEOSOPHY THE RELIGION OF JESUS. By Alex. Fullerton. 2d.

THEOSOPHY AND OCCULTISM. By G. R. S. Mead, B.A. (*Cantab.*) 2d., post free, 2½d.

YOGA, The Science of the Soul. By G. R. S. Mead. 2d., post free, 2½d.

MAN, His Origin and Evolution, according to Theosophic Philosophy. By Herbert Coryn and George Spencer. 1d., post free, 1½d.

A SHORT GLOSSARY OF THEOSOPHICAL TERMS. Compiled by Annie Besant and Herbert Burrows. 1d., post free, 1½d.

THEOSOPHY, AND THE LAW OF POPULATION. By Annie Besant. 1d., post free, 1½d.

KARMA. By Snowden Ward. 1d.

THE THEOSOPHICAL MAHÂTMÂS. By Alexander Fullerton. 2d., post free, 2½d.

INTRODUCTION TO THEOSOPHY. Annie Besant. 3d.

MEANING AND USE OF PAIN. do. do. 3d.

DEVOTION. do. do. 3d.

THEOSOPHICAL GLEANINGS OR NOTES ON "THE SECRET DOCTRINE." 6d.

STUDIES IN THE SECRET DOCTRINE. 4d.

THEOSOPHY IN QUESTIONS AND ANSWERS. By Annie Besant. 3d., post free, 3½d.

THEOSOPHY AND CHRISTIANITY. By Annie Besant. 2d., post free, 2½d.

INTRODUCTION TO THEOSOPHY. By Annie Besant. 3d., post free, 3½d.

EVOLUTION ACCORDING TO THEOSOPHY. By Katharine Hillard. 6d., post free, 6½d.

SPIRITUALISM CONSIDERED IN THE LIGHT OF THEOSOPHY. Post free, 1d.

SOME MODERN FAILINGS. By Che-Yew-Tsang. 3d., post free, 3½d.

THEOSOPHICAL SIFTINGS.

PLEASE QUOTE VOL. AND NO., NOT NAME.

FIRST YEAR.

No.		Price.
1.	—Theosophy and the Churches - - - -	2d.
2.	—Psychic Bodies and Soul-Survival - - -	2d.
3.	—Philosophie de Mystik - - - -	3d.
4.	—The Theosophical Movement, etc. - - -	2d.
5.	—What is Matter and What is Force? etc. - - -	2d.
6.	—Reincarnation, etc. - - - -	3d.
7.	—Practical Occultism, etc. - - - -	4d.
8.	—Epitome of Theosophical Teachings - - -	3d.
9.	—Keeley's Secrets - - - -	6d.
10.	—Nature-Spirits or Elementals - - - -	4d.
11.	—The Higher Science - - - -	2d.
12.	—Was Jesus a Perfect Man? - - - -	2d.
13.	—The Hebrew Talisman - - - -	6d.
14.	—Selflessness, Thelyphthoria, and Taro - - -	3d.
15.	—Swedenborg Bifrons; or Swedenborg, the New Church Sect, and the Theosophical Society - - - -	3d.
16.	—Theosophical Concepts of Evolution and Religion - -	3d.
17.	—Inter-Relation of Supernatural Phenomena and the Ethics of Theosophy - - - -	4d.
18.	—Parabrahm - - - -	6d.

SECOND YEAR.

No.		Price.
1.	—Alchemy - - - -	2d.
2.	—Possibilities of Scientific Prophecy, etc. - - -	3d.
3.	—The Curse of Separateness, etc. - - -	3d.
4.	—The Old Wisdom-Religion, now called "Theosophy," etc. -	6d.
5.	—Universal Brotherhood, etc. - - - -	3d.
6.	—The Valley of the Quest, etc. - - - -	3d.
7.	—Theosophy and Modern Socialism, etc. - - -	6d.
8.	—Theosophia; or Divine Wisdom, etc. - - -	3d.
9.	—What Theosophy and its Society should be, etc. - -	3d.
10.	—A Sketch of Theosophic Organization - - -	3d.
11.	—What is Theosophy? - - - -	3d.
12.	—The Life of a Christian Philosopher - - -	3d.
13.	—Let us be Practical, etc. - - - -	3d.
14.	—Acquired Habits, Psychometry - - - -	6d.
15.	—Thought Transference, etc. - - - -	3d.
16.	—Theosophy and Orthodoxy, Part I., etc. - - -	3d.
17.	—Theosophy and Orthodoxy, Part II., etc. - - -	3d.
18.	—The Soul according to the Qabalah - - -	3d.

Third Year.

1.—Capital Punishment, etc. - - - 3d.
2,—Practical Suggestions for Daily Life. etc. - - - 3d.
3.—Summary of Bertram Keightley's Lectures in America - 3d.
4.—Theosophical Symbology, etc. - - - - 3d.
5.—Vivisection, etc. - - - - 3d.
6.—Theosophy and Modern World Problems, the Rosicrucians - 3d.
7.—Have Animals Souls? (by H. P. Blavatsky). - - 6d.
8.—Masters of Wisdom - - - - 4d.
9.—Inauguration of the European Headquarters - - 6d.
10.—The Scientific Importance of Dream - - - 3d.
11.—Reincarnation, The Tarot Cards - - - 3d.
12.—Cremation (by Franz Hartmann, M.D.) - - - 3d.
13.—National Karma; Atlantis - - - - 3d.
14.—The Mayas and Quiches - - - - 3d.
15, 16.—Keely and Science - - - - 6d.
17.—Theosophy and Practical Occultism; Simon Magus - 3d.
18.—Treatment of Criminals and Lunatics - - - 3d.

Fourth Year.

1.—Why is Theosophy True? - - - 3d.
2.—A Sketch of Theosophy - - - - 3d.
3.—The Ancient Magic Crystal and its Connection with Mesmerism - - - - 4d.
4.—Topics in Reincarnation - - - - 3d.
5.—The Mystery of Pain, the Meaning of Sorrow, and the Hope of the World - - - - - 3d.
[6.—Marriage in the Mineral World - - - - 3d.
7.—The Kingdom of Light and the Secret of Love (by Franz Hartmann, M.D.) - - - - - 6d.
8.—Eastern Psychology - - - - - 3d.
9.—Alchemy in the Nineteenth Century (by H. P. Blavatsky) - 3d.
10.—Light from the East - - - - - 6d.
11.—True Science, or Keely's Latest Discoveries - - 6d.
12.—Theosophy and Theosophical Christianity - - 3d.
13.—The Septenary Nature of Consciousness - - - 3d.
14, 15.—Topics in Karma - - - - - 6d.
16.—An Elementary Note on the Seven Principles - - 4d.
17.—The Mission of Theosophy - - - - 3d.
18.—A Glance at the First Three Races of mankind - - 3d.

Fifth Year.

1.—Keely's Progress - - - - - - 6d.
2.—Theosophy and Art - - - - - - 3d.
3.—Spiritualism in its Relation to Theosophy - - 4d.
4.—Heaven and Hell - - - - - - 3d.
5.—The Secret Doctrine and the Higher Evolution of Man - 3d.

6.—The Philosophy of Self-Knowledge - - -	3d
7.—Theosophy and the Hebrew Scriptures - - -	3d
8.—Convention Speeches, 1892. - - - -	6d
9.—The World as Subject and Object - - -	3d
10.—Astral Bodies - - - - -	3d.
11.—Faith by Science - - - - -	6d.
12.—Man's Relation to the Phenomenal World - -	3d.
13.—The Hermetic Philosophy - - - -	3d.
14.—The Mystic Side of Christianity - -	3d.
15.—Theosophical Conceptions of Compassion and Affection -	3d.
16.—Some Anomalies in the Biblical Views of the Constitution of Man. - - - - -	3d.
17, 18.—Studies in Buddhism - - - -	6d.

SIXTH YEAR.

1.—The Bhagavad Gîtâ - - - - -	3d.
2—Priesthoods - - - - -	3d.
3.—On Gems - - - - -	3d.
4.—Theosophy and Modern Science - - -	3d.
5.—Death - - - - - -	3d.
6.—Psychic and Noetic Action - - - -	3d.
7.—Emerson and Theosophy - - - -	3d.
8.—Egyptian Belief - - - - -	6d.
9.—Occult Physiology - - - - -	3d.
10.—Notes on Nirvâna - - - - -	6d.
11.—Evolution - - - - -	3d.
12.—Legend of the Grail. Karma - - - -	3d.
13.—The Zodiac - - - - -	3d.
14.—A Word on Man, his Nature, and his Powers - -	3d.
15.—Christian Rosenkreuz and the Rosicrucians - -	3d.
16.—Man and his Creators - - - - -	3d.
17.—Occultism Past and Present - - - -	3d.
18.—Theosophy the True Basis of True Socialism - -	3d.

SEVENTH YEAR.

1.—The Moral Aspect of Karma - - - -	6d.
2.—An Hour of Borderland Occultism - - -	4d.
3.—Neo-Platonism - - - - -	3d.
4.—Life Eternal - - - - -	3d.
5.—Theosophy and the Alcohol Question - - -	3d.
6.—The Language of Symbols - - - -	4d.
7.—Consciousness - - - - -	3d.
8.—The Myth of Prometheus - - - -	4d.
9.—Plethora - - - - -	3d.

10.—Philosophy and Ethics of the Zoroasters - - - 3d.
11.—The Doctrine of the Resurrection - - . 4d.
12.- The Cambridge Platonists - - - - 3d.
13.—Extracts from Synesius on Providence - - - 3d.
14.—The Reincarnating Ego. The Evolution of Man - - 3d.
15.—An Essay on the Beautiful. By Plotinus. Translated by Thomas Taylor - - - - - 6d.
16, 17.—The Cave of the Nymphs. By Porphyry. Translated by Thomas Taylor - - - - - 6d.
18.—Devachan - - - - - - 6d.

Vols. 1, 2, 3, 4, 5, 6, 7, bound in cloth. 7s. 6d. net. each.

MAGAZINES.

LUCIFER. Founded by H. P. Blavatsky. Co-Editors, Annie Besant, G. R. S. Mead. Annual subscription, 17s. 6d.; single copies, 1s. 6d. each.

THE THEOSOPHIST. Conducted by Colonel Olcott. Annual subscription, 20s.; single copies, 2s. each.

THE PATH. Edited by W. Q. Judge. Annual subscription, 8s.; single copies, 1s. each

THE IRISH THEOSOPHIST. Annual subscription, 3s. 6d.; single copies, 3d. each

THE VAHAN. Annual subscription, 2s. 6d.; single copies, 3d. each.

THE THEOSOPHICAL FORUM. Single copies, 3d. each.

JOURNAL OF THE MAHA-BODHI SOCIETY. Annual subscription, 5s.

JOURNAL OF THE BUDDHIST TEXT SOCIETY (quarterly). Annual subscription, 10s.

THE ORIENTAL DEPARTMENT OF THE EUROPEAN SECTION (issued at intervals). Price, post free, 3½d. each

BOOK NOTES—THEOSOPHICAL, OCCULT, ORIENTAL AND MISCELLANEOUS. Annual subscription 2s.

Covers for binding *Lucifer* and *Theosophical Siftings*, 1s. 6d. each.

TRACTS.

WHY YOU SHOULD BE A THEOSOPHIST. By Annie Besant.
THEOSOPHY AND THE SOCIETY OF JESUS. By Annie Besant.
THEOSOPHY AND ROMAN CATHOLICISM. By Herbert Burrows.
WHAT THEOSOPHY IS. By Annie Besant.
THEOSOPHY AND OCCULTISM. By a Hindu F.T.S.
THEOSOPHY AND ITS PRACTICAL APPLICATION.

Four shillings per 100. One penny each

LEAFLETS.

THEOSOPHY.
THEOSOPHIC LIFE.
KARMA.
REINCARNATION,

One shilling per hundred.

PHOTOGRAPHS.

	£	s.	d.
H. P. Blavatsky (large size) - - - -	1	10	0
Annie Besant (large panel) - - - -	1	1	0
" " - - - -	0	10	6
" " - - - -	0	7	6
H. S. Olcott " - - - -	0	7	6
Convention Group 1893 (unmounted) - - -	0	7	6
" " 1894 " - - - -	0	7	6
The Dweller on the Threshold. R. Machell - -	0	5	0
The Birth of a Planet. " - - -	0	5	0
The Path " - - -	0	5	0
H. P. Blavatsky (cabinet) - - - -	0	2	0
Annie Besant " - - - -	0	2	0
The Countess Wachtmeister (cabinet) - -	0	2	0
W. Q. Judge " - - -	0	2	6
H. S. Olcott " - - -	0	2	0
Herbert Burrows " - - -	0	2	0
H. P. Blavatsky and H. S. Olcott - - -	0	0	6

Postage and packing extra.

A LARGER CATALOGUE OF IMPORTANT BOOKS RELATING TO THEOSOPHY, THE OCCULT SCIENCES, ORIENTAL RELIGIONS, ETC., SENT POST FREE ON APPLICATION.